DICKENS

OLIVER
TWIST

NOTES

COLES EDITORIAL BOARD

Bound to stay open

Publisher's Note

Otabind (Ota-bind). This book has been bound using the patented Otabind process. You can open this book at any page, gently run your finger down the spine, and the pages will lie flat.

ABOUT COLES NOTES

COLES NOTES have been an indispensible aid to students on five continents since 1948.

COLES NOTES are available for a wide range of individual literary works. Clear, concise explanations and insights are provided along with interesting interpretations and evaluations.

Proper use of COLES NOTES will allow the student to pay greater attention to lectures and spend less time taking notes. This will result in a broader understanding of the work being studied and will free the student for increased participation in discussions.

COLES NOTES are an invaluable aid for review and exam preparation as well as an invitation to explore different interpretive paths.

COLES NOTES are written by experts in their fields. It should be noted that any literary judgement expressed herein is just that — the judgement of one school of thought. Interpretations that diverge from, or totally disagree with any criticism may be equally valid.

COLES NOTES are designed to supplement the text and are not intended as a substitute for reading the text itself. Use of the NOTES will serve not only to clarify the work being studied, but should enhance the reader's enjoyment of the topic.

ISBN 0-7740-3342-8

© COPYRIGHT 1997 AND PUBLISHED BY
COLES PUBLISHING COMPANY
TORONTO - CANADA
PRINTED IN CANADA

Manufactured by Webcom Limited
Cover finish: Webcom's Exclusive **DURACOAT**

CONTENTS

Charles Dickens: Life and Works

Charles John Huffam Dickens was born February 7, 1812, in Portsea (now Portsmouth), England. He was the second of eight children born to Elizabeth (Barrow) Dickens and John Dickens, a poorly paid navy pay office clerk. From the age of two to five years, Charles lived with his family in London, where his mother tutored him in English and Latin. From the age of six to ten years, the family lived in Chatham, where Charles attended a school run by William Giles, the son of a Baptist minister. In 1823, the family moved to London, where Charles spent much time exploring the streets that later became scenes for his novels.

As John Dickens found himself unable to meet his mounting debts (like the unforgettable Micawber of *David Copperfield*), Elizabeth Dickens attempted to supplement her husband's income by opening a private school for young children — but her efforts were unsuccessful. Charles went to work in a blacking warehouse when he was only 12 years old. Early in 1824, John Dickens was imprisoned for debt at Marshalsea (notoriously portrayed in *Little Dorrit*). Elizabeth Dickens and the six youngest children joined him in the debtors' prison while Charles stayed in a rooming house in London, supporting himself on his shilling-a-day earnings. Dickens described his work in this way:

> It was to cover the pots of paste blacking first with a piece of white paper and then with a piece of blue paper, to tie them round with a string, and then to clip the paper close and neat all round until it looked as smart as a pot of ointment from an apothecary's shop.

> He had to do his work in front of the window and people used to stop and look at him. Dickens hated this and used to shudder with embarrassment. The situation was worsened by the fact that, as in *David Copperfield*, the other boys were rough.

> No words can express the secret agony of my soul, as I sank into this companionship. I worked from morning till night with common men and boys, a shabby child.

I know that I tried but ineffectually not to anticipate
my money and make it last through the week. I know I
have lunged through the streets insufficiently clad and
unsatisfactorily fed. I know but for the mercy of God,
I might easily have been, for any care that was taken of
me, a little robber or a little vagabond.

All this left a deep impression on Dickens' mind and was
reflected in his works. Most of the important child characters in
his stories had similarly unpleasant childhoods.

While he was employed at the blacking factory, lodgings of a
sort were provided for him. But for the rest, Dickens had to support
himself on a paltry wage of six shillings a week. With no
money to go anywhere and little to do, Dickens spent his leisure
hours wandering around London, an experience that was to serve
him well in the writing of his novels. In them, he described not
only the imposing places in London, but also the grimy back
alleys such as those inhabited by the frightening villain in *Oliver
Twist*, Bill Sikes. Dickens acquired a knowledge of London and
London life that was second to none, but the blacker side of London
life is more prominent in his novels — the slums in *Bleak
House* rather than the fashionable promenades of the West End.

Luckily for Dickens, his father was released from the Marshalsea
after six months, after inheriting a legacy that enabled
him to pay off his debts. Soon after his release, Mr. Dickens
quarrelled with the owner of the blacking factory and Charles
was dismissed. He went back to school happily, this time to the
Wellington Academy at Hampstead. One of his schoolmates
said that he was a handsome, curly-headed lad, full of life and
fun, and probably was connected with every mischievous prank
in the school. During this time he began to write tales that he
passed around among the other boys. He also developed a love
of amateur theatricals that remained with him all his life, for he
was a born actor.

Dickens' love of amateur theatricals led him to arrange
private shows for his family and friends. He longed to be a professional
actor. He might have fulfilled this ambition later on in
his early twenties had not a bad cold prevented him from going
to an interview with the stage manager of Covent Garden
(although at that time he had begun to do rather well as a
reporter and gave up the idea).

When Dickens left school, at the age of 15, he found himself as a lawyer's clerk, tending to the petty cash ledger. His immediate ambition soon changed, and he decided to become a reporter, as his father had done on leaving prison. With characteristic determination, he set out to fit himself for the job, teaching himself shorthand and studying in the evenings at the British Museum. As a result of this, Dickens obtained a job as a shorthand writer in the Courts of Doctors Commons (the law courts; "Doctors" refers here to Doctors of Law). Once again, Dickens was to use his experiences later in his novels. In *A Tale of Two Cities* and *Great Expectations*, the Inns of Court are used, while in *Pickwick Papers* and again in *A Tale of Two Cities*, there are well-known trial scenes. He himself worked in Gray's Inn and it was there that he became familiar with the ways of lawyers and the neighborhood of Chancery, which he describes as if he knew every stone of its courts and alleys.

When Dickens was 22, he thought it would be more exciting to be a general reporter, and he obtained a job on the *Morning Chronicle* at a salary of five guineas a week. He was sent all over the country, from Edinburgh to Exeter. He thoroughly enjoyed every moment of it. As a boy, he had often gone cold and hungry, but now he could arrive at night at a comfortable hotel, order a good meal and relax in front of a good fire. But a reporter's life in those days was not all fun and games, for Dickens was a conscientious worker and his work came first.

> I have been in my time belated on miry byroads towards the small hours 40 or 50 miles from London in a wheelless carriage with exhausted horses and drunken postboys, and have got back in time for publication, to be received with never-to-be-forgotten compliments by my editor.

It was Dickens' custom to draw his characters from life and place them in situations and surroundings with which he was familiar. In the same way, many of the exciting scenes in his novels arose from Dickens' experiences as a newspaperman. Anyone who has read the descriptions of scenes such as the shipwreck at Yarmouth in *David Copperfield* will realize what a fine reporter he was. This fact did not escape his editors, and before long he was being kept in reserve to be sent on important emergency assignments at a moment's notice. His reports, like his novels, had vividness, gusto and a sense of humor, so different from the colorless, factual reports in so many newspapers of the day.

In 1833, Dickens published in the *Monthly Magazine* his first work of fiction, *Dinner at Poplar Walk* (later reprinted as *Mr. Minns and His Cousin*). The next year, Dickens published additional sketches in this journal, as well as in the *Morning Chronicle* and its affiliate, the *Evening Chronicle*. In 1836, all of these short pieces were published together as *Sketches by Boz*. Dickens used the pen name of "Boz" (suggested by his brother's pronunciation of "Moses" while he had a cold). During 1836-37, under the sponsorship of the Chapman and Hall publishing firm, Dickens wrote the serial, *Pickwick Papers*, a humorous, episodic narrative that became widely popular.

Dickens always wrote from experience or deep knowledge of his city. He was a thorough and accurate observer. If he had but a scanty knowledge of his story, he would take great pains to obtain fuller details at first-hand. For example, before writing *Nicholas Nickleby*, which was published in 1838, he researched his facts by traveling to Yorkshire, where he visited various boarding schools under the pretext of looking for a school for the son of a friend. One school he visited was the Bowes Academy, for he had read that its headmaster had been in court for cruelty. Here he found the brutal atmosphere that is recaptured in the descriptions of Dotheboys Hall in *Nicholas Nickleby*.

In April of 1836, Dickens married Catherine Hogarth, whose father was a music critic and editor of the *Evening Chronicle*. In the late 1830s, Dickens established himself as a social reformer when, as editor of the monthly, *Bentley's Miscellany*, he published *The Mudfrog Papers* and *Oliver Twist* (1837-39). The latter work presented a critical picture of the workhouse and the foundling home, thereby attacking both the Poor Law and the conduct of charitable institutions. During this period, Dickens was working at a characteristically feverish literary pace, producing such lesser works as *Sketches of Young Gentlemen* (1838) and *Sketches of Young Couples* (1840).

In 1840, Dickens edited the weekly, *Master Humphrey's Clock*, for which he wrote the serials *The Old Curiosity Shop* (1840-41) and *Barnaby Rudge* (1841). Since international copyright regulations were not yet established, Dickens' works were pirated in America. Perhaps out of revenge, he wrote *American Notes* (1842), which contained unfavorable comments on American manners, institutions and the practice of slavery. Further criticisms were directed at Americans in *Martin Chuzzlewit* (1843-44), a comic satire.

The first of Dickens' Christmas books, *A Christmas Carol*, appeared in 1843, followed by *The Chimes* (1844), *The Cricket on the Hearth* (1845), *The Battle of Life* (1846), and *The Haunted Man* (1848).

From 1844 to 1846, the Dickens family (now grown to five) lived alternately in Italy, Switzerland and France. Out of this itinerant period came *Pictures from Italy* (1844-45) and *Dombey and Son* (1846-48), which attacked family pride and the worship of wealth. On his return to England in 1847, Dickens organized an amateur theatrical company in which he served as manager and principal actor. In 1851, the group was joined by Wilkie Collins, a prominent playwright and novelist who became Dickens' close friend and collaborator.

David Copperfield (1849-50) reflected a semi-autobiographical account of Dickens' own rise from obscurity to fame. Departing from the farcical caricatures and exaggerations of his earlier work, it marked an artistic advance for the author. In 1850, Dickens and William Henry Wills started *Household Words*, a weekly journal taking a reformist political position. In it appeared *A Child's History of England* (1851-53), *Bleak House* (1852-53), which attacked the Chancery courts and the slums around Chancery Lane, and *Little Dorrit* (1855-57), a satire of Victorian England.

Dickens' love of acting was one of the great passions of his life. At Christmas in 1853, Dickens gave his first public readings in Birmingham Town Hall, in aid of the establishment of a Birmingham and Midland Institute, which would give greater educational opportunities for the working people. There was a natural choice of what to read in *A Christmas Carol*. Dickens wrote to the organizers:

> There would be some novelty in the thing as I've never done it in public, though I have in private and, if I may say so, with a great effect on the hearers.

His reading that night was so successful that he was asked to give a second reading three days later. This he consented to do on condition that it should be a working people's night with cheap seats that working people could afford.

> I never saw, nor do I suppose anyone ever did, such a moving sight as the working people's night. There were 2,500 of them there and a more delicately observant audience it is impossible to imagine. They lost nothing, misinterpreted nothing, followed everything closely, laughed and cried with the most delightful correctness.

Dickens frequently visited Birmingham. On one occasion, he was there with some friends after a visit to Shakespeare's birthplace at Stratford and Dr. Johnson's at Lichfield. They stopped longer than expected and ran short of cash. They were forced to pawn their gold watches with a Birmingham jeweler. His friends thought this hardly dignified, but Dickens could afford to laugh at it. He probably remembered the times as a boy when he had been sent to the pawnshop after dark so that the neighbors would not see, but now, with wealth and fame behind him, it was just a huge joke, for who cared who knew?

When he was a boy in Chatham, Dickens had dreamed of buying Gad's Hill Place near Rochester. Once again, he was able to fulfil a childhood ambition, for, in 1856, he bought it and lived there most of the time from 1860 until his death.

It gave him a thrill that the house was situated on Shakespeare's Gad's Hill, mentioned in *Henry VI*, Part I. Dickens put up a plaque on the first-floor landing:

> This house, Gad's Hill Place, stands on the site of Shakespeare's Gad's Hill, ever memorable for its association with Sir John Falstaff in his noble fancy.

Gad's Hill Place was generally full of company, fun and laughter. Later on, Dickens bought the meadow behind the house to be used for cricket and other games. A nearby cricket club was allowed to make the meadow its own ground. He also sponsored athletic competitions for which he provided the prizes. Once again he was successful in his ventures, for one year 2,000 people turned up.

The joy of Gad's Hill Place was marred for Dickens and his wife by growing marital unhappiness. By 1858, a legal separation was agreed upon and his sister-in-law, Georgina Hogarth, managed Dickens' household affairs from then until his death. Concurrent with the separation, and due to a rift with the part owners of *Household Words*, Dickens and Wills dissolved the periodical and launched in its place, *All the Year Round*. To ensure the magazine's success, the first issue began the weekly serial of *A Tale of Two Cities*, followed by other serials including *The Uncommercial Traveller* (1860), which was a commentary on foreign and domestic issues, and *Great Expectations* (1860-61), another semi-autobiographical novel.

Dickens gave public readings from 1859 to 1868 in London, Scotland and North America, adding substantially to his income. His last completed novel was *Our Mutual Friend* (1864-65), another social satire. This was followed by two shorter works published in America by James Thomas Fields: *A Holiday Romance* (1868), which was a children's story, and *George Silverman's Explanation* (1868), which sneers at dissenters.

Back at Gad's Hill Place in 1870, Dickens began work on a suspense tale, *The Mystery of Edwin Drood*. Shortly after completing his sixth instalment, he collapsed in the dining room of his home. He died the next morning, June 9, at the age of 58. His request for a simple grave near his last home was ignored and he was buried at Westminster Abbey.

The characters he created have become personal friends to his many readers through the years. Dickens has given us a warm, rich and full world, a world such as it is, full of the good and the bad, but always full of hope for the future. He was a man of the ordinary folk. It was about ordinary folk that he wrote and to them he gave the rich world of his imagination.

Historical Background to the Novel

Oliver Twist is a very topical novel in that its contents are directly relevant to the period in which it was written. It is, therefore, important to know something of conditions in England at that time, and particularly of conditions under the Poor Laws which were the object of Dickens' main attack.

England in the Early 19th Century

Dickens, born in 1812, grew up at a time when Britain was undergoing the most far-reaching social transformation in her history. Industrial and urban growth were inevitably creating enormous social problems. The population was increasing rapidly; in 1811 the census figure was 12 million, in 1851 it had risen to 21 million. There was a sweeping movement of workers towards the towns. Landowners became fewer and richer, as improved methods of agriculture came into use. The nation as a whole was at a peak of prosperity and apparent greatness but her facade concealed underlying depths of poverty, crime and squalor.

Between rich and poor — the upper and lower class — lay a great gulf. But in this "age of reform" there was an increasing awareness of social abuses. By mid-century, problems were being faced and solutions proposed, in almost every area of life: in local government, lawcourts, prisons, factories, schools, workhouses. And Dickens himself — no matter how he may be criticized for a lack of constructive suggestion — was part of this reforming movement, and nowhere more so than in *Oliver Twist*, which contains his blistering attack on Poor Law institutions.

Poor Laws

Under Queen Elizabeth I, laws had been made which provided for the relief of those who could not support themselves. The old, the sick, the lame and the blind would be taken care of at home; orphans were to be boarded out and then apprenticed to a trade; vagrants were to be sent to Bridewells ("houses of correction"). In theory, work was to be found for the able-bodied or "sturdy beggar" and gradually relief was extended to the able-bodied poor as well.

Special buildings were set up, originally intended as places where the poor would be employed under supervision — and thus they were known as workhouses — and, by an Act passed in 1722, the poor could be compelled to live and work in these buildings, in order to receive relief. In other words, either a pauper lived in the workhouse or he got no relief. This was known as the "workhouse test." At first there were separate institutions for the different needs of children, old people or those who were mentally or physically sick. But gradually the workhouse came to contain a mixture of able and disabled alike, and by the end of the 18th century it had become a symbol of utter degradation. In most workhouses, conditions were atrocious; husbands were separated from wives, children lacked proper care, diseases were rife, food was inadequate. Such were still the prevailing conditions when Dickens wrote *Oliver Twist*.

In the late 18th century, laws had been passed which would allow "outdoor relief" to the able-bodied, so that workhouses should house only the old or disabled. Originally it was intended that a minimum wage should be fixed for laborers but instead, the "Speenhamland system" was devised, whereby relief, based on the current price of bread, was given in addition to wages. This system, introduced in time of crisis (when England was at war with France) was effective enough in the short run, but led to a general weakening of the independence and self-respect of laborers and to an increase of pauperism.

The early 19th century movement for poor law reform was faced with two main problems:

(1) An alternative solution had to be found for the practice of outdoor relief, which had become both wasteful and corrupt. Somehow the able-bodied poor were to be excluded from workhouses, and given a chance to regain their independence.

(2) The whole system of administering relief needed to be overhauled. The parochial set-up — as described below — was no longer adequate.

The Parish

The parish was the main unit of local government in rural England. As the country became industrialized, the parochial system became increasingly inadequate.

In 1835 there were about 15,635 parishes in England and

Wales. The parish came under the higher jurisdiction of the county, in which "justices of the peace," chosen from land-owning families, held the reins of civil administration. These justices of the peace were responsible for imposing the compulsory rates (the "poor rate") and for appointing local overseers who in turn administered actual relief.

There were four chief parochial officers. The *Church-warden*, responsible to religious authority (Bishop or Archdeacon), supervised church affairs, and acted as a trustee of common property. The *Constable*, a forerunner of local policeman, his original duty was the supervision of beggars and poor. The *Surveyor of Highways* supervised road repairs, statute labor, etc. The *Overseer* worked closely with the churchwardens and administered rates, etc.

The *parish beadle* was an officer of inferior status, as may be seen in *Oliver Twist*. However, he was able to wield considerable power on a small scale. The beadle's original function was like that of a town crier; he had to proclaim meetings, and was also expected to keep order in church and punish petty offenders.

Any or all of these officers in a particular parish might be (and frequently were) unsuitable for their jobs, because of their own lack of education, experience or responsibility. They were elected, usually in annual meetings of the "vestry" or assembly of parishioners or their representatives and their positions were both unpaid and compulsory.

This, then, was the administrative system upon which the welfare of thousands depended. It was not an easy one to reform.

In 1832 a commission was appointed to study the whole question of poor law reform. On the basis of proposals made by this commission, the New Poor Law of 1834 came into being. This was not so much a new law, as an amendment to the old one. Its main features were:

(1) A central authority was created, the Poor Law Commissioners, who were given full powers to control local administration.

(2) Parishes were to be grouped into unions.

(3) Parish officers were to be replaced (for the purpose of

administering relief) by elected local bodies known as Boards of Guardians. One such board is portrayed in *Oliver Twist*. These boards would supervise paid officials such as the matron of the workhouse.

(4) Outdoor relief to the able-bodied was to be discontinued, on the grounds that it discouraged independence and wasted public money. (Compare the discussion between Mr. Bumble and Mrs. Corney in *Oliver Twist*, Ch. 23).

There is no doubt that these measures of 1834 were excellent in intention, but disastrous in effect. There were several important questions raised by the new laws. Dickens singled out a few for attack in *Oliver Twist*:

(1) the harsh regime of workhouses, with special regard to diet;

(2) the utter neglect of the needs of pauper children;

(3) the inefficiency and inhumanity of such officials as Mr. Bumble and Mrs. Corney.

There has been much discussion among scholars as to whether Dickens was attacking the old poor law or the new; but, as K.J. Fielding points out, "The novel was never intended as an attack on mere institutions, but on the *spirit behind them*, which remained largely unchanged."

Dickens did, however, make a specific attack on the *philosophy* underlying the new poor laws (see his discussion of the Board of Guardians in Ch. 2). This philosophy was based upon the doctrine of Thomas Robert Malthus, whose *Essay on the Principle of Population* (first published in 1798) had put forward the view that population tended to increase beyond the means of subsistence. (He formulated this view as follows: population, if unchecked, will increase in geometrical progression, whereas the means of subsistence will increase in arithmetical progression.) This idea leads, obviously, to the discouragement of increasing population. Malthus' view was that the increase would be effectively discouraged by the "natural checks" of misery, vice and moral restraint, hence the Malthusian opposition to all forms of charity. As Dickens put it (*Oliver Twist*, Ch. 2): "So they established the rule that all poor people should have the alternative . . . of being starved by a gradual process in the house, or by a quick one out of it."

The Writing of *Oliver Twist*

Dickens began to write *Oliver Twist* — his second novel — in response to popular demand. But whereas in *Pickwick Papers* he had given his readers an essentially comic treatment of life and manners, in *Oliver Twist* he changed his tone. He said it was "necessary for his own satisfaction" that he attempt something new and more serious. What he produced in *Oliver Twist; or, The Parish Boy's Progress* — the subtitle is significant — was a combination of social satire and grim melodrama. Even the comedy in this novel is always dominated by the reforming zeal which underlies it.

Throughout his career, Dickens exhibited tremendous indignation against social evils: poverty, oppression and injustice, as exemplified in schools, prisons, workhouses and the like. He hated the inhumanity of institutions, and satirized the people who represented institutions, kept them going or who were blind to their faults. Thus in *Oliver Twist* his most powerful and passionate writing occurs in the first 11 chapters, where he portrays a world in which "life is cheap, suffering general and death welcome" — the world of workhouses and thieves' dens, which are the product of pauperism and neglect.

Dickens' purpose in writing *Oliver Twist*, then, was twofold:

(1) to confront his readers with the dreadful predicament of the poor and the inadequacies of existing institutions;

(2) to meet his readers' demand for another novel which would entertain them as *Pickwick* had done.

As to the subject matter of the story itself, we do not know much about how it occurred to Dickens, as he left no record of its origin. It is not, like *David Copperfield*, autobiographical. A few of its characters (Rose Maylie, Mr. Fang, Fagin) were drawn from living models, but for the most part this novel sprang from Dickens' imagination. In making a small boy the central figure, he was setting a precedent for several of his later novels. As for the topical and violently controversial issue — the 1834 Poor Law amendment — which he chose as the main target of his satire, Dickens' own years as a parliamentary reporter had increased both his knowledge of the problem and his scepticism about the attempted solution.

Characters in the Novel

The Artful Dodger: Nickname of Jack Dawkins.

Barney: A young Jew who is a waiter at the Three Cripples, a tavern that the criminals frequent. He is involved in the burglary at the Maylie house.

Charley Bates: A member of Fagin's gang of thieves. He is characterized by his constant laughter.

Mrs. Bedwin: Elderly housekeeper to Mr. Brownlow. She develops a fondness for Oliver.

Bet: A young girl who is part of Fagin's gang.

Blathers: An incompetent police officer from London who investigates the burglary at Mrs. Maylie's.

Morris Bolter: An assumed name that Noah Claypole uses when he becomes part of Fagin's gang in the city.

Brittles: A simple-minded general handyman who is employed by Mrs. Maylie.

Mr. Brownlow: A respectable gentleman who meets Oliver during the pick-pocket incident. He is kind to Oliver and offers him a home. Eventually, he adopts Oliver.

Bull's-eye: Bill Sikes' dog who accompanies his master everywhere.

Mr. Bumble: The unkind and pompous parish beadle who is one of Oliver's first tormentors. Later, he marries Mrs. Corney and becomes the workhouse master.

Mrs. Bumble (née Mrs. Corney): The matron of the workhouse who marries the beadle and causes his life to be a misery.

Charlotte: A kitchen servant to the local undertaker in the workhouse town. Later, she runs away with Noah Claypole and works for Fagin in London.

Tom Chitling: One of Fagin's "hopeful pupils" who is recently out of prison.

Noah Claypole: A charity-boy a few years older than Oliver. In the workhouse town, he is employed by the undertaker. Later, in London, he becomes one of Fagin's thieves and calls himself Morris Bolter.

Toby Crackit: An associate of Bill Sikes. He is a burglar who works with Oliver in a robbery attempt at the Maylie house.

Jack Dawkins: Also known as the Artful Dodger. A skillful pickpocket who is the favorite of Fagin. He brings Oliver to London.

13

Dick: A small, sickly boy who is Oliver's only friend at the juvenile parish house run by Mrs. Mann in the workhouse town.

Duff: A partner to Blathers, he is an equally inept police officer.

Fagin: An old and unpleasant Jewish fence who runs a small gang of petty thieves in London. He takes Oliver in and tries to train him as a pickpocket.

Mr. Fang: A cruel magistrate in London to whom Oliver is brought when he is arrested for picking Mr. Brownlow's pocket.

Agnes Fleming: Oliver's young mother who died when he was born.

Rose Fleming: The rightful name of Rose Maylie. Sister to Agnes and Oliver's aunt.

Mr. Gamfield: A chimney sweep in the workhouse town. He is a cruel man who tries to secure Oliver as his apprentice.

Giles: Mrs. Maylie's butler who is attributed with wounding Oliver during the robbery.

Mr. Grimwig: A gruff but kind-hearted friend of Mr. Brownlow.

Kags: An old convict who is in hiding with members of Fagin's dispersed gang near the end of the story.

Edward Leeford: Monks' real name.

Edwin Leeford: A friend of Mr. Brownlow. Father to both Monks and Oliver.

Mr. Losberne: A neighborhood doctor and friend to the Maylies. He cares for Oliver when the boy is shot during the burglary.

Mrs. Mann: A selfish woman who runs the parish house for small children in the workhouse town.

Harry Maylie: Handsome son of Mrs. Maylie. He eventually becomes a clergyman and marries Rose.

Mrs. Maylie: An elderly widow whose house is broken into by thieves. She offers Oliver a home after he is wounded.

Rose Maylie: Adopted niece of Mrs. Maylie. She is a gentle, young girl who marries Harry Maylie. She turns out to be Oliver's aunt.

Monks: A sinister criminal who is associated with Fagin. He is Oliver's half-brother whose real name is Edward Leeford.

Nancy: A young girl who is part of Fagin's gang. She has mercy on Oliver and is later murdered by her lover, Bill Sikes.

Old Sally: The old pauper who attends Oliver's birth in the workhouse, and who later reveals information about Oliver's mother.

Bill Sikes: A brutal housebreaker and associate of Fagin. He is Nancy's lover who later murders the girl for her efforts to help Oliver.

Mr. Sowerberry: The parish undertaker in the workhouse town. He takes Oliver on as an apprentice.

Mrs. Sowerberry: Wife of the undertaker. A heartless woman who resents and abuses Oliver.

Plot Summary

Oliver Twist is an orphan born into intense poverty. He is raised by parish officials in a corrupt system of starvation and neglect. His early years pass uneventfully in different workhouse locations.

At the age of nine, Oliver is made an apprentice to the local undertaker. After many weeks of abuse and unhappiness, he runs away to the city of London.

On his journey, he meets the Artful Dodger who is a pickpocket in the city. The Dodge takes Oliver to Fagin, an old man who is a fence and also runs a gang of young thieves in a seamy part of London.

Oliver is trained to be a pickpocket but manages to get away from the thieves during a street incident. He is arrested for picking the pocket of a gentleman who then takes pity on the boy. Oliver is brought to live with Mr. Brownlow and, for some time, spends many happy days for the first time in his life.

Meanwhile, the thieves are planning to get Oliver back. They kidnap him and keep him prisoner. Despite their efforts to make him a hardened criminal, Oliver is desperate to escape. On a particular robbery attempt, Oliver is involved and becomes wounded by a gunshot. The burglars abandon him for dead in a ditch.

He is eventually rescued by the very family the thieves unsuccessfully tried to rob. Mrs. Maylie, the mistress of the house, and her niece, Rose, offer Oliver a new and kind home.

Great mysteries are associated with Oliver's past and there are unexplained connections between him and some of his benefactors.

As the thieves plot to recapture Oliver, Nancy, a young girl among them, feels sorry for him and risks her life to help him. Through her efforts, the mysterious story of Oliver's background is unfolded. She is murdered for her betrayal of the thieves.

The gang of thieves is pursued and eventually destroyed. Oliver's parentage and his connection to Mr. Brownlow and Rose Maylie is revealed. Far from being a poor, workhouse orphan, Oliver is the son of fine parents who left him a considerable inheritance. When the evil obstacles in the path of his claim are finally removed, there is great happiness as Oliver, at last, achieves his rightful place in the world of goodness and mercy.

Chapter By Chapter Summaries and Commentaries

NOTE: All quotations are from *Oliver Twist*, Charles Dickens, New American Library.

CHAPTER 1

Summary

In this first chapter, the birth of the protagonist, Oliver Twist, is recorded. It is an occasion unmarked by any signs of happiness. An unfortunate and unmarried young woman, too poor to receive proper medical care, has been brought to a workhouse after collapsing on the street. By the next day, she has given birth to a boy child. This birth is attended only by a hired doctor and an old woman who works in a drunken stupor. The young mother asks to see her child and then dies.

For a few anxious moments it appears that the infant will not survive. Then he begins a loud crying that announces his intention to live. The doctor departs for home and the old woman dresses the baby in dirty and well-used clothes.

Commentary

Since the novel opens with the birth of the main character, the author makes it clear that he is going to tell the story of Oliver Twist in chronological order, so that the reader is witness to his development.

The opening chapter is carefully constructed so that it is anonymous and impersonal. Only the newborn child is given a name and he is born into impoverished circumstances.

During Dickens' lifetime, England was undergoing great social reforms. Urban and industrial growths were creating far-reaching social problems. The gap between the upper and lower classes was unbreachable. There were laws to assist the poor and infirm but they were inadequate and outdated. The Victorian workhouse was an institution created to house the poor, the orphaned and the disabled. People, unable to care for themselves, were sent to workhouses for relief. Originally, these workhouses were intended to be places where the poor could be employed under supervision. Eventually they became disorganized and mismanaged establishments that housed masses of unwanted humanity. Conditions in these places were atrocious. With *Oliver Twist*, Dickens was drawing attention to the deplorable conditions in the poor law institutions.

It is in one of these workhouses that Oliver is born and left orphaned. The details of his surroundings are deliberately vague. The town is not named, nor is the workhouse, and the date of his birth is not given. Even the child's mother is nothing more than a "pale face" and a "faint voice," a representative of the unfortunate class of abject poverty, doomed to suffering and a dismal death.

Oliver's entrance into the world is not a joyous event. The child, referred to as "the item of mortality," is already disadvantaged at his birth. The world for Oliver, and for all unfortunates of his class, will be a place "of sorrow and trouble." When the old woman wraps him in worn-out and tattered clothes, it is evident that his station in life is inevitable and unchangeable:

> . . . he was badged and ticketed, and fell into his place
> at once — a parish child — the orphan of a workhouse
> — the humble half-starved drudge — to be cuffed and
> buffeted through the world, — despised by all, and
> pitied by none.

Through his mastery of subtle irony and understatement, Dickens is able to comment effectively on the horrible social conditions. In describing the birth of Oliver, whose existence is so precarious in the first moments of life, Dickens indirectly shows the reader how unfortunate the infant's circumstances are. Attended only by an indifferent doctor and an old pauper who is herself an inmate of the workhouse, Oliver draws his first breaths. The reference the author makes to the absence of devoted and anxious grandmothers and aunts serves to underline the lonely and friendless entrance the child makes into this world. When he mentions that the attentions of such caring relatives would have "killed [him] in no time," the underlying meaning is that they would have killed him with kindness. The reality of the situation is thus emphasized. Oliver, instead, has only the indifference of the doctor who sees the newborn child as "troublesome" and the drunken incompetence of the old woman.

When Oliver's mother asks to see her baby before dying, the old woman scolds her for her negative attitude. The old woman says, "Think what it is to be a mother," as if to remind the dying woman of the many joys and pleasures that exist in being a workhouse mother. But Dickens gives us a more accurate picture of what raising children in poverty is like. The old woman has had 13 children, but only two have survived in the squalor of the workhouse. It is an unpleasant reminder of the class of life to which Oliver has been born, a life in which he will be "left to the tender mercies of churchwardens and overseers." With the suggestion that perhaps the child might have "cried the louder" if he had been aware of this, the chapter ends.

CHAPTER 2

Summary

The child, Oliver, is kept at the workhouse for most of the first year of his life. The workhouse, however, does not have suitable facilities for the care of an infant so Oliver is transferred to a privately-run house for juveniles. This place is managed by Mrs. Mann who pockets most of the allowance money she is paid for the care of each child. The children, in turn, are uncared for and hungry. Many die from this system of neglect but the few investigations that are made by the governing board reveal only death by natural causes or accident.

In this heartless environment Oliver grows to be a fragile and hungry nine-year-old. On his birthday, he and two companions are beaten and locked in the cellar as punishment for being hungry. On this day, Mr. Bumble, the parish beadle (a petty official in the social system), arrives at Mrs. Mann's house. The proprietress is careful to release Oliver and his companions from the cellar before she admits Mr. Bumble.

Bumble is a fat and officious man with an inflated sense of his own importance. He accepts a drink of gin from Mrs. Mann and they discuss their responsibilities for the care of the parish orphans. Then Bumble explains the reason for his visit. The authorities of the parish have been unable to locate information on Oliver's mother or father. By order of the board, Oliver is to be returned to the workhouse where he was born. Oliver, who has been somewhat cleaned up, is brought in to Mr. Bumble and they depart for the workhouse.

Later that day, Oliver is summoned before the board that controls and regulates parish workhouse policies. The intimidated child appears in front of a group of severe men who question and instruct him on his behavior. They explain that he is to be educated and learn "a useful trade." The next morning he will begin his new job of picking oakum (a process of unraveling old rope).

Oliver settles into this new life of deprivation and hardship. All the boys in the workhouse are constantly hungry. Their meager diet of thin gruel (oatmeal), an occasional onion and some bread is insufficient for growing boys. After several months of this, one of the beggar boys decides to do something. He declares he is so hungry that he will eat one of his smaller companions. After a hasty discussion, the other boys draw lots to decide who should ask for more food. The unpleasant task falls to Oliver. That evening at supper, when the gruel is being dished out, Oliver asks for more. The simple request becomes an incident. Mr. Bumble is summoned and later reports the occurrence to the board. As a result of his impudence, Oliver is put into confinement. Immediately the board posts a notice in the neighborhood offering five pounds to any person who will take the ungrateful child as an apprentice. Meanwhile, the board members are so distraught by the incident that one of them ventures to predict that such an insolent upstart as Oliver will no doubt come to a violent end.

Commentary

True to the suggestion in Chapter 1 about Oliver's treatment at the hands of "churchwardens and overseers," the reader sees that life in the lower class is a difficult one.

Since the workhouse is not equipped to care for infants, Oliver is sent, while still a baby, to live with Mrs. Mann. The cruel and selfish nature of the woman is exposed when Dickens says that "she knew what was good for children" and, at the same time, "what was good for herself." The children in her care are deprived of food while she pockets the money that has been allotted for that purpose. Naturally, the death rate in such a system of neglect is very high. Dickens cites instances of these children dying from neglect or from horrible accidents. He takes care to point out the absurd gestures of the governing board to regulate the deplorable conditions. Members of the board never see the true situation since, before they arrive for inspections, the house is warned of their visit. The children are, of course, made presentable and the board can then only report on the favorable conditions. Even the few inquiries that are set up into the alarming death rate are fraudulent. The board uses testimony of the parish beadles and of doctors under contract to the board who swear that the deaths are natural. The fact that they are caused by starvation is overlooked.

When Mr. Bumble comes to remove Oliver from Mrs. Mann's, it is clear to the reader that these two parish officials are very similar. Both are heartless and inhumane to the children. They are both well-fed while the paupers starve. The great hypocrisy they indulge in when they discuss the orphans is rendered ridiculous by the author. As they contentedly drink gin, they discuss their own senses of importance.

Dickens' characterization of Bumble is a famous one. A beadle was a very insignificant minor official within the parish system. Bumble, however, has a different view of his importance. He is pompous and impatient, expecting deferential treatment from Mrs. Mann. Priding himself on his "oratorial powers" he nevertheless mispronounces many words, like "porochial." He is also proud of himself for having "inwented" the name of Oliver Twist. He explains grandly to Mrs. Mann how he came upon the name while using the board's policy of following the alphabet to choose names for the orphans.

Once Oliver has been transferred back to the workhouse, Dickens carefully portrays the appalling conditions. For the orphans it is a life of more deprivation and further intimidation. They are mistreated, insufficiently fed and punishment is severe. Yet they are expected to be grateful to this social system that is killing them through neglect.

Treating the subject of workhouses with tongue-in-cheek humor, Dickens elaborates on the inhumanities of the system. Married couples are separated, children taken away from their parents and the poor are given a choice of how they will starve to death: quickly out on the streets or slowly in the workhouse. The only drawback to this system is the high cost of the undertaker's services since so many of the inmates die.

In contrast to the thin Oliver and his starving companions in the workhouse, the employees of the parish are all presented as well-fed and healthy. Mr. Bumble is overweight, as are the gentlemen of the board and the master of the dining room who spoons out small portions of watery gruel for the boys.

Kindness and caring do not exist in the world of the workhouse. Children are beaten, locked in dark places, intimidated and kept in a state of perpetual fear. The people who are assigned the care of these children are portrayed as austere, selfish and heartless. Their reactions to the incident of Oliver's requesting more food is displayed as being ridiculous and exaggerated.

CHAPTER 3

Summary

As punishment for asking for more food, Oliver is put in solitary confinement for one week. During the long days he cries and, at night, he huddles in a corner, frightened and trembling. His only outings consist of being flogged before the other boys at supper time and of being exhibited at prayers as an example of bad behavior to the others.

One day, Mr. Gamfield, a chimney sweep, is leading his donkey-cart past the workhouse. Gamfield is worried about the sum of five pounds which he needs for rent. As he walks along and thinks, he is occupied with beating his donkey. Suddenly he notices the posted bill advertising Oliver's services as an apprentice.

Gamfield decides he needs just such an apprentice. On his way to inquire, he is met by Mr. Limbkins, one of the members of the parish board. Shortly, he is taken before the other members and they negotiate on the amount of the reward offered for Oliver. A price of just over three pounds is finally agreed on. Mr. Bumble is sent to retrieve Oliver from his imprisonment and to clean him up.

When Oliver appears before two magistrates who must approve the final papers for his apprenticeship, he is upset by the proceedings and terrified by the appearance of Mr. Gamfield. One of the magistrates is very old and half-blind. He is about to sign the documents when he happens to observe the frightened look on Oliver's face. Instead of signing the papers, the old gentleman questions Oliver on his feelings about the apprenticeship. Oliver, in desperation, pleads with the magistrate to do anything with him rather than send him away with the chimney sweep. The old man, who is kind-hearted, considers Oliver's words and decides not to approve the apprenticeship. Oliver is sent back to the workhouse on the magistrate's orders.

The members of the board are shocked by the decision and appalled at Oliver's continued ingratitude. They predict an even more horrible future for him and arrange to have a new notice posted about the child's availability.

Commentary

For the audacity of requesting more food, Oliver is locked in "a dark and solitary room" and left for a week. His terror and loneliness are relieved only when he is removed to be humiliated in front of the other boys. The punishment is certainly in excess of the offence.

The financial needs of the chimney sweep coincidentally match the reward offered by the board. For a while, it appears that Oliver's fate will proceed from bad to worse as Gamfield bargains with the board over the child's fate. The overt cruelty of Gamfield to his poor donkey is a clear measure of the man's character. Even in his fright, Oliver can recognize the danger of being turned over to such a man. That realization prompts him to plead with the magistrate.

Coincidence figures again in Oliver's fate in the ruling of the magistrate. Had it not been for the old man's failing eyesight, he would have located the inkstand and duly signed the necessary papers. Instead, he encounters the look of fear on Oliver's face. It is a rare moment of benevolence in the destiny of the child. He is spared worse cruelty because of chance.

CHAPTER 4

Summary

The members of the board consult about the possibility of sending Oliver to sea aboard a trading ship. They send Mr. Bumble to make inquiries.

On his return, Mr. Bumble encounters Mr. Sowerberry, the parish undertaker. As they have a friendly talk about the profits of the undertaker's business, Mr. Bumble asks if Sowerberry knows of anyone looking for an apprentice. The undertaker finally decides to take Oliver for himself.

Again that evening, Oliver is led before the board to be informed of his new position. This time, he displays no emotion and remains silent. The gentlemen of the board assume he is becoming "a hardened young rascal" when actually his youthful spirit is being beaten out of him by repeated abuse.

Mr. Bumble takes Oliver to his new employer. On the way, Oliver pleads for some kindness and understanding. He cries and says, "I am a very little boy, sir; and it is so . . . lonely." Even the hardened Bumble is temporarily moved by the child's pleas.

When they arrive at the undertaker's establishment, Oliver is inspected by Mr. and Mrs. Sowerberry. The lady of the house is not pleased with the prospect of having to feed and clothe Oliver. Orphans, she says, "always cost more to keep, than they're worth." Then she sends him downstairs to be fed by the kitchen girl, Charlotte. Mrs. Sowerberry orders that he be given the table scraps that they were saving for their dog, Trip. Oliver, hungry as usual and not used to eating meat, devours the mess appreciatively.

When he is finished, Mrs. Sowerberry leads him upstairs to show him where he will sleep. His bed is under a counter, among the coffins.

Commentary

Again, Oliver's destiny seems to be directed by chance. Had Mr. Bumble not encountered Mr. Sowerberry at the gate of the workhouse, perhaps Oliver would have been sent to sea where the captain of the ship would, most likely, "flog him to death." The wishfulness of the gentlemen of the board for this fate for Oliver emphasizes their cruelty.

During the friendly conversation between Bumble and Sowerberry, the reader is made to see how the deaths of the paupers in the workhouses are a commercial asset. When a pauper dies, the workhouse population is reduced and, at the same time, the parish undertaker makes money. The flippant remarks of the two men demonstrate society's attitude toward the unfortunate lower class.

In an incident of great irony, Sowerberry admires the button that Bumble is wearing on his jacket. Bumble proudly explains that it is "the Good Samaritan, healing the sick and bruised man." The beadle was awarded the button by the board. The situation is highly ironic because neither man is associated with the concept of "healing." One of them actively participates in mistreating poor people and the other profits from the effects of the mistreatment when those people die.

As decisions are made about Oliver's future, Dickens deliberately presents the boy as already being reduced to a pathetic state. Since the reader is acting as witness to Oliver's development, Dickens wants to make it clear that the boy is suffering at the hands of the parish. When he is brought before the board to hear of their decision regarding his life, he is passive and silent. As the author explains, he "was in a fair way of being reduced, for life, to a state of brutal stupidity and sullenness by the ill-usage he had received."

On their journey to the undertaker's, Oliver is described as "tremulous," "piteous" and "helpless." In his fear of what will become of him in his new employ, he cries and clings to Bumble, holding "the hand which held the well-known cane." In his desperation, he begs for pity from the beadle. The reader can gauge the depth of Oliver's despair by the momentary softening of Mr. Bumble who "hemmed three or four times in a husky manner." Later, when Oliver is fed by Mrs. Sowerberry, the reader witnesses the heart-breaking scene in which Oliver eagerly devours leftover table scraps intended for the dog. A final play on the reader's sympathy is made in this chapter when the undertaker's wife leads Oliver to his bed among the coffins.

In his new life, Oliver does not seem to be much better off than he was in the workhouse. Here, among unfriendly strangers, he is to make his home. His surroundings are "dark" and "dismal." His employer's wife has "a vixenish countenance." The kitchen girl is described as "slatternly." Even Mr. Sowerberry has a face that is "not naturally intended to wear a smiling aspect." The man's only warmth appears to be in connection with his business, which he treats with a light heart.

CHAPTER 5

Summary

Oliver is understandably distressed about having to sleep among the coffins. Everything around him in the dim light seems frightful and threatening. As he goes to sleep, he wishes one of the coffins could be his so he could be at rest in a peaceful churchyard.

25

The next morning, he is awakened by the sound of kicking at the door of the shop. An abusive voice shouts to Oliver to let him in. When Oliver opens the door, he finds a rough-looking youth whose name is Noah Claypole. This lad is a charity-boy and he makes it clear to Oliver that a charity-boy outranks a workhouse orphan. Referring to Oliver only as "Work'us," Noah orders Oliver to remove the shutters from the windows. As he obeys, Oliver breaks a pane of glass. The older boy is delighted because Oliver will be punished by Sowerberry.

In the kitchen, Charlotte pays special attention to Noah's breakfast but gives Oliver only "stale pieces." Noah continues teasing Oliver and Charlotte joins in. The two of them laugh and treat Oliver with scorn.

Nearly a month passes and one evening Mr. Sowerberry has an idea about Oliver that he timidly tries to put to his wife. After some sharpness on her part and some apologetic begging on his, she finally consents to let him speak of his idea. He explains that Oliver has a melancholy expression that would be suitable for a "mute" at children's funerals — someone who is paid by the undertaker to be a mourner.

With his wife's grudging approval, Sowerberry has a chance the very next day to have Oliver "initiated into the mysteries of the profession." Bumble arrives to inform the undertaker of the death of a poor woman named Bayton. This death causes Bumble some consternation since the husband of the woman who died refused to administer medicine provided by the parish. He is in such a fury that he fails to inquire after Oliver.

Sowerberry takes Oliver and they set out to find the Bayton house. They eventually locate it in a dirty and miserable street in a very poor section of town. Even the rats in this area are "hideous with famine." Here they meet the husband and mother of the woman who has died. The husband is distraught with grief and anger. He explains that his wife became deathly ill while he was away in prison for begging. When he was released from prison, his wife's condition was critical from starvation and she died before he could do anything to help. The old woman, on the other hand, regards the present situation as an opportunity that is "as good as a play." Because of the death in the family they are all entitled to some extra food from the parish and to some special consideration.

The burial takes place the next day. It is a cold day with drizzling rain and the whole affair is dismal and unpleasant. The dead woman's husband falls down in a faint by his wife's grave and the old woman is hysterical because she must give up the cloak she was loaned for the funeral.

When Oliver and Sowerberry return to the shop, Oliver is hesitant to express much enthusiasm for his new trade. Sowerberry consoles him saying "you'll get used to it in time," but Oliver is not convinced.

Commentary

Oliver's treatment at the hands of Noah Claypole illustrates the existence of exploitation in all levels of society. Because of his advantage of being a charity-boy (one who has parents but still receives parish help) in comparison to Oliver's workhouse status, Noah is belligerent and demanding. The older boy is clearly a bully who delights in the misfortunes of others.

The death of a woman in the parish gives the author a chance to portray the appalling conditions of poverty. The hunger of his wife caused a man to go begging. For this "crime" he is sent to prison. In his absence, his wife's condition worsens and she eventually dies. Bumble is indignant at the circumstances involved in this particular death. The family refused to give her medicine that was delivered, without diagnosis, by the doctor's apprentice. Her death is nothing more than an irritation to the insensitive beadle. He regards the family as ungrateful and troublesome. He fails to recognize that the parish actually contributed to the poor woman's death.

In his first experience with a funeral, Oliver is naturally timid. The squalor of the dead woman's family and the pathetic funeral rites combine to impress him with the indignities of poverty. He is unconvinced when Sowerberry tells him he will get accustomed to it. The boy is, by nature, too sensitive to become hardened by the sight of suffering.

CHAPTER 6

Summary

After a month of probationary service, Oliver is formally apprenticed to the undertaker. He is gaining in experience and is extremely successful as a hired mourner. At the same time, he is getting a chance to observe human behavior. He watches as people at funerals undergo dramatic emotional transformations. Oliver is glad to see people recover so rapidly from their grief. He is learning about hypocrisy.

Sowerberry is pleased with Oliver's performance and treats him well. But the others in the household are not as kind to Oliver. Noah Claypole is jealous of Oliver's promotion to professional mourner. Charlotte follows Noah's example and also treats Oliver unkindly. Mrs. Sowerberry dislikes Oliver simply because her husband likes him.

One day, while Oliver and Noah are in the kitchen alone, Noah makes a special attempt to torment Oliver of whom he is so jealous. Unable to reduce Oliver to tears with his usual taunts, threats and physical abuses, Noah resorts to personal comments about Oliver's mother. Oliver responds to this attack. He has tender and sensitive feelings about his mother who died, as he believes, "of a broken heart." Having found Oliver's weak spot, Noah persists in his badgering. When he makes a comment that Oliver's mother was "a regular right-down bad 'un," Oliver can take no more. In a fury of resentment and anger, Oliver attacks the much larger but cowardly Noah, knocking him to the floor. The bully's cries attract the attention of Mrs. Sowerberry and Charlotte who rush in to save Noah. The three of them manage to subdue Oliver and to bestow a considerable number of blows on him before they lock him in the cellar. Oliver's rage is still unchecked and he kicks angrily at the door. Meanwhile, Mrs. Sowerberry is in a distracted state, worrying that Oliver is dangerous to all of them. Since Mr. Sowerberry is absent, she sends Noah to find Mr. Bumble to help them with this problem.

Commentary

Oliver's persecution by Noah continues. The older boy is jealous of Oliver and reacts with typical unkindness. Charlotte and Mrs. Sowerberry are equally abusive to Oliver and for similarly unfounded reasons. They are all possessed of a simple nature tinged with jealousy and cruelty.

When Noah finds Oliver's weak spot, the bully focuses his nasty attention there. As Dickens points out, it is behavior characteristic of "many small wits" who get "personal" when they actually intend "to be funny."

This attack by Noah prompts a new response in Oliver. He is transformed from the "mild, dejected creature that harsh treatment had made him" into a "glaring" and "roused" opponent. When he knocks Noah to the floor, he is inspired by a passionate defence of his mother.

The cowardly cries of the bully are also characteristic of the charity-boy. Older and larger than Oliver, he is easily frightened by genuine anger. The combined efforts of Noah, Charlotte and Mrs. Sowerberry in subduing the infuriated little boy are comical in their intensity. It takes three people, and the promise of Mr. Bumble's arrival, to bring Oliver's new "spirit" under control.

CHAPTER 7

Summary

Noah hastens to the workhouse to find Mr. Bumble. When he sees the beadle, the charity-boy puts on a noisy display of distress and pain to convince Bumble of Oliver's violence. Bumble is suitably impressed and so is the gentleman of the board who is also present. He and Bumble listen to Noah's exaggerated account and then agree that Bumble should accompany Noah to Sowerberry's and administer a good flogging to the boy.

At the undertaker's, Oliver remains defiant, even in the threatening presence of the dreadful beadle. He continues to kick at the cellar door and to shout for his release. Mr. Bumble, astonished by Oliver's audacity, is unsure of how to handle the situation. He suggests that the problem has come about because Oliver has been too well-fed. He explains:

> You've raised a artificial soul and spirit in him, ma'am, unbecoming a person of his condition. . . . What have paupers to do with soul or spirit? It's quite enough that we let 'em have live bodies. If you had kept the boy on gruel, ma'am, this would never have happened.

His practical solution is to keep Oliver locked up without food for a few days in order to tame him.

At this point in the negotiations, Mr. Sowerberry arrives

and is informed of the incident. Without hesitation, the undertaker drags Oliver out of the cellar and confronts him. Oliver is unrepentant and defiant of his tormentors. When he accuses Mrs. Sowerberry of lying, the undertaker has no alternative but to punish Oliver. He is locked up for the rest of the day, until he is sent to bed.

Only when he is alone among the coffins does Oliver give in to his feelings. With no one to watch him or taunt him, he falls on his knees and cries. After a while, he begins to make plans to run away. He gathers his few possessions together and waits for the first light of morning.

As soon as the sun is up, Oliver makes his escape from the house where he has endured so much suffering. He decides to stop on his way at Mrs. Mann's where he spent his childhood. Oliver encounters Dick, a sickly orphan who was his companion in misery there. Oliver confides in Dick and the little boy gives him encouragement and a blessing. It is the first time anyone has ever invoked a blessing on Oliver and it is a kindness he will never forget.

Commentary

Bumble and the board gentleman are easily deceived by Noah's dramatic account of Oliver's actions. The fact that these two men believe the larger boy's interpretation of the beating he received from the smaller Oliver, reveals their readiness to expect the worse from a workhouse orphan.

When Bumble arrives at the undertaker's, he summons up all of his effectiveness to quell the fury of the small boy. When Oliver remains defiant even in the beadle's ominous presence, Bumble is reduced to "mute astonishment." His perception of his own authority exceeds the reality of it.

Bumble's explanation for Oliver's behavior is an absurd reversal of the truth. He contends that Oliver's defiance is a direct result of being overfed. The opposite is pathetically apparent. If Oliver had received any kindness at all and some proper nourishment, he would not have to resort to such overt resistance. As it is, the meanness of his life has endowed him with "soul or spirit," an attribute quite unrecognizable to a man like Bumble.

Oliver's decision to run away is an extension of his newfound ability to fend for himself. With this realization comes a desire to remove himself from the place where he has been so cruelly mistreated. It is ironic that his only supporter is a young child who is dying from starvation and neglect. With Dick's blessing, Oliver sets out into a new life.

CHAPTER 8

Summary

By eight o'clock that morning, Oliver has put almost five miles behind him and the place of his birth. Fearful all the while of being followed and returned to the undertaker, he alternates between running and hiding behind hedges. At a stile in the road, he stops to rest and ponder his future.

He notices a stone marker that informs him that the great city of London is 70 miles away. He decides to make that his destination. He recalls old men in the workhouse speaking of London and of how a "lad of spirit need [not] want in London." Oliver decides it is "the very place for a homeless boy."

With no food or money, he sets off on his journey. During the days, he begs food and water when he dares to and, at night, he sleeps outside without shelter. Cold, hungry and alone, he travels for seven days until he comes to the town of Barnet. As he stops to rest, too tired to beg, he realizes that he is being watched by "one of the queerest-looking boys" he has ever seen. This lad is about Oliver's age with a "flat-browed" face and "little, sharp, ugly eyes." He is very short, standing only four and a half feet, and has bowed legs. In addition to his peculiar features, the boy is wearing man-sized clothing which hangs loosely on him and he has a "roystering and swaggering" attitude of a much older person.

This boy, whose name is Jack Dawkins, strikes up an acquaintance with Oliver and then treats him to a meal. Oliver is impressed with the strange qualities of his new benefactor and Jack, in turn, is impressed with Oliver's naivete.

Since Oliver's destination is London, Jack offers to accompany him and to introduce him to a "'spectable old genelman" who will provide Oliver with free food and lodging.

As their conversation becomes more friendly, Jack discloses that he is "a peculiar pet and protégé" of the old gentleman. He also admits that among his friends in London he is called "the artful Dodger."

Oliver has no alternatives and is glad to have the offer of some help. He accepts Jack's proposal. He resolves to himself that if the situation in London with the "old genelman" is an acceptable one, he will detach himself from Jack's disreputable acquaintance.

Once night has come, young Dawkins leads their way into London. Traveling through many city streets, the Dodger brings Oliver to an area near Field Lane. Oliver notices his surroundings and realizes he has never seen anything dirtier or more wretched. Around him the air is foul, the street is muddy and ragged people are "wallowing in filth." Just as Oliver is considering running away from the Dodger, they come to a broken down and dirty house. After the Dodger gives a password, they are admitted into a room "perfectly black with age and dirt" where Fagin, "a very old shrivelled Jew," is preparing some food. He is a villainous-looking character with a "repulsive face . . . obscured by a quantity of matted red hair." Sitting at a table is a group of boys of about the same age as the Dodger. They are drinking and smoking pipes and acting like "middle-aged men."

When Oliver is introduced, Fagin and his "hopeful pupils" are anxious to be friendly. Under the pretense of shaking Oliver's hand and helping him with his few belongings, they are actually checking for any valuables he might be carrying.

Fagin then serves supper to the boys. Afterwards, he gives Oliver a hot drink spiced with gin. The exhausted boy immediately falls asleep.

Commentary

For the first time in the novel, a specific location is identified. When Oliver arrives in Barnet, a town north of London where he meets the Artful Dodger, the action is moving closer to the city of London. It is in London that Oliver will begin his new life. It is also London that Dickens wants to draw the reader's attention to. It is a metropolis made up of all kinds of people. Oliver's introduction to it, and the reader's, exposes the poverty and squalor that exist on a larger scale in the city.

It is again the element of chance that is directing Oliver's fate. When he encounters the Dodger in Barnet, he is on his way to the seamy underworld of London. Through the Dodger he is introduced to the infamous Fagin and his gang of young thieves.

The character of Fagin is based on a well-known figure of Dickens' day. The Jewish fence (a person who buys and resells stolen goods) was a notorious criminal considered to be worse than a thief because he encouraged others to steal for him.

The Dodger and the boys in Fagin's gang are mere children but their appearance and behavior cause them to resemble much older men. It is Dickens' way of suggesting that their lives of poverty and crime have deprived them of their childhoods. They seem to have grown old in the atmosphere of evil.

It is into this environment that Oliver is brought. He has left behind the misery and cruelty of the workhouse town in the hope of finding a new and better life. It appears at this point, however, that he has traded off one miserable style of life for another. Oliver had told his friend, Dick, at the end of Chapter 7, "I am going to seek my fortune, some long way off. I don't know where." His entry into the disreputable world of Fagin marks the first phase of the "fortune" he was seeking. Because of his worldly innocence, which the Dodger brands as being "green" or inexperienced, he is a perfect candidate for the criminal activities of Fagin, the Dodger and his associates.

CHAPTER 9

Summary

The next morning Oliver awakes very late after a sound sleep. While he lies in bed, half awake and half asleep, he observes the activities of Fagin. The old Jew, satisfied that Oliver is sleeping soundly, locks the door and takes from a hiding place in the floor small boxes which contain many pieces of valuable jewelry. While he gloats over these treasures, he speaks aloud to himself, commenting on the hanging of five thieves who went to their deaths without giving information on Fagin and his gang.

When the old man glances at Oliver, he sees with alarm that the boy is awake and watching. For a few moments, Fagin becomes aggressive and malicious. He picks up a knife from the table and holds it menacingly. Only when Oliver assures him that he has just opened his eyes does the old man replace the knife and resume his genial attitude. He explains to Oliver that the "pretty things" in the boxes are his "little property," his life's savings for his old age. But, while Oliver gets up to wash, the box vanishes from view.

Shortly after, the Dodger returns, accompanied by a hearty-natured young man whom Oliver had noticed the night before. He is introduced as Charley Bates and Oliver notices that he laughs a great deal for no apparent reason. Over breakfast, they show Fagin the "work" they have accomplished that morning. They have been to a public execution and their pick-pocketing exploits have gained them two wallets and some pocket-handkerchiefs. Oliver, unaware of the true nature of their "work," does not grasp the meaning of their activities or of their discussion.

After breakfast, Fagin dresses up as a gentleman and lets the Dodger and Bates practise their pick-pocket techniques on him. While this is repeatedly rehearsed, two young women arrive. Named Bet and Nancy, they are "not exactly pretty," but they are heavily made up, carelessly dressed and are "free and agreeable in their manners."

This group spends some cheerful time together drinking and talking until Bates suggests that it is time to "pad the hoof." Fagin distributes some money to the four of them and they leave.

To Oliver's innocent questions about the activities of the foursome, Fagin replies with only vague answers. Instead, he encourages Oliver to model himself after the Dodger who will one day be "a great man." Then, without explaining what he is doing, Fagin gives Oliver his first lesson in picking pockets.

Commentary

Dickens is providing the reader with more insight into the world of London criminals. It is serious business that Oliver has inadvertently become involved in. Young boys his own age are hanged for their participation in thefts of items which fences like Fagin are willing to buy.

Dickens also takes the opportunity to satirize the code of honor that exists among thieves. Fagin is extremely satisfied that five of his associates were hanged and that they never "peached" or informed on Fagin and his whereabouts.

Fagin's true nature emerges briefly when he realizes that Oliver is watching him inspect his horde of treasures. The "merry old gentleman" momentarily turns into a fierce and scowling cutthroat who brandishes a knife at a child when his hiding place has been found out. It is clear that his kind and thoughtful behavior is a facade covering his vile and vicious temperament.

Dickens provides the reader with an inside look at the workings of the underworld. The language of Fagin's gang is a careful reproduction of the slang of criminals of that time. The practice of picking pockets is a well-rehearsed art. The conversation that Fagin has with the Dodger and Bates about their "work" at the execution illustrates a criminal technique that was prevalent in Dickens' day. Pickpockets at public executions found conditions most favorable to their trade. At the moment when the attention of the crowd was fixed on the platform, the pickpockets were able to conduct their business freely and easily. Such is clearly the case for the Dodger and Bates when they return to Fagin with their accumulation of stolen property. The two women who are introduced in this chapter are not the "ladies" that Dickens suggests they are. They, too, are involved in the illegal and dangerous activities associated with Fagin. Their appearances are coarse and slovenly. Just as with the young boys who work for Fagin, these two girls have become cheapened and degraded by their experience with evil.

Oliver, at whom the others laugh because of his naivete, is naturally bewildered and unable to comprehend the occupations of these seemingly pleasant and kind-hearted people. He is a bright and sensitive child, anxious to be accepted and treated with kindness. He is unaware that both his cleverness and innocence make him a perfect candidate for Fagin's manipulations.

CHAPTER 10

Summary

Oliver stays in Fagin's room for some time. He is kept busy with removing the identifying stitches from stolen handkerchiefs and with daily pick-pocketing rehearsals.

Tired of being captive indoors and conscious of the cruelty in Fagin's nature, he requests that he be sent out with the other boys to "work." Fagin finally agrees to let him go with the Dodger and Bates when their supply of stolen goods begins to diminish.

As the three of them set out, Oliver is amazed at the leisurely and sauntering pace the other boys take to go to their "work." To Oliver's unsuspecting mind, their casual behavior and petty pranks on the street lead him to believe that they are not going to work at all.

Suddenly their attitude changes and they become furtive and attentive. They point out to Oliver "a very respectable-looking personage" who is examining a book by a bookstall. This old gentleman is well-dressed and thoroughly preoccupied with his reading. To the Dodger and Bates he is a perfect target.

When, in a few moments, the Dodger removes the gentleman's handkerchief and hands it to Bates, Oliver suddenly realizes the significance of his life with Fagin and the boys. He understands completely that they are thieves and he is terrified by his association with them. Following the example of the Dodger and Bates who are making a fast getaway, Oliver starts to run. At that moment, the old gentleman turns, realizes his handkerchief is gone and spots Oliver. His cries of "Stop thief!" attract the attention of people in the street, and soon Oliver is being pursued by an angry mob which includes his two companions. Finally, he is stopped by a blow from a "great lubberly fellow," and lies helpless and bleeding in the street. The crowd gathers around him, hostile and curious. When the old gentleman arrives, he reluctantly identifies Oliver as the boy who picked his pocket. He is the only person in the crowd who has any sympathy or concern for the bedraggled child lying on the pavement. The man accompanies Oliver and a policeman away from the scene, as the Dodger and Bates slip away into the crowded street.

Commentary

Until now, Dickens has maintained an atmosphere of sustained irony. All along in Oliver's association with Fagin, the reader has been aware of the criminal activities going on around him. Because of his trusting nature and innocence, only Oliver has been unsuspecting of the true occupations of his benefactors.

When the Dodger steals the handkerchief from the gentleman at the bookstall, Oliver recognizes the true nature of his companions' "work." He is horrified at his connection with such unlawful characters. Now that he understands the mysterious activities that went on in Fagin's room, he is anxious to escape.

As Oliver makes his run and is chased by an ever-increasing

throng of angry citizens, Dickens uses the incident to illustrate a basic human trait. Mankind, he says, has "a passion *for hunting something.*" The enthusiasm and ferocity with which the townspeople pursue the terrified and helpless child are meant to reveal the cruelty of a mob mentality. When even the Dodger and Bates join in the chase, Dickens is showing typical criminal morality.

For the few paragraphs in which Oliver is hunted down, Dickens adds to the excitement and tension of the episode with his masterful use of language. As he describes the swelling excitement in the streets, punctuated by the outraged cries of "Stop thief!," his use of diction and structure provide a parallel of sound and activity that echoes the actual movement of the angry citizens.

When Oliver is stopped by a heavy blow from a large man, he is left hurt and helpless on the street, subject to the jeers and curious stares of the crowd. These people have no sympathy for the frightened and injured child. Only the old gentleman whose pocket was picked shows any sign of compassion.

The pickpocket episode illustrates an ironic reversal in effect in Oliver's life. The boys who are responsible for the theft become part of the mob that pursues the boy who is innocent. Oliver, whose morality would not allow him to participate in a criminal act, is hounded and run to the ground like an animal. The proportions of justice seem uneven.

CHAPTER 11

Summary
Oliver is led to a neighboring police station accompanied by the old gentleman and the indignant crowd. When they arrive, Oliver is searched and locked into a small and dirty cell.

While they are waiting for the magistrate to appear in his office, the old gentleman, named Mr. Brownlow, is intrigued by some familiarity he sees in Oliver's face. Try as he might to recall faces from his past, he is unable to place the resemblance he notices. So, being of an "absent" character, he spends his time reading the book he has carried with him since the incident at the bookstall.

After a short wait, Mr. Brownlow is called into the office of Mr. Fang, the presiding magistrate. In the room is a frightened

Oliver, confined in a wooden pen. Mr. Brownlow tries to explain that he is not sure that Oliver is the guilty party but he is overruled by the nasty-tempered and sharp-tongued Mr. Fang. Following many unnecessary questions by the magistrate and countless interruptions in the proceedings, Oliver, who is sick and trembling with fear, is sentenced to three months' hard labor. Brownlow, meanwhile, is indignant and mortified by the conduct of the magistrate. He checks his temper only because it might harm Oliver's case. Just as the magistrate is sentencing Oliver, the owner of the bookstall hurries into the office to testify on Oliver's behalf. He was a witness to the theft and verifies that Oliver was "amazed and stupefied by it."

Upon hearing this evidence, Mr. Fang decides to release Oliver and to chastise Mr. Brownlow for having acquired his book under "very suspicious and disreputable circumstances."

When an outraged Brownlow and the bookstall owner reach the street, they find Oliver unconscious on the pavement, pale and trembling. They call for a coach, place Oliver inside and drive away.

Commentary

The ruthless Mr. Fang is Dickens' caricature of inhumane justice. This sadistic man whose authority decides "the liberties, the good name, the character, almost the lives, of Her Majesty's subjects, especially of the poorer class," is presented as an overbearing tyrant. He is described as "stiff-necked" and "stern" and has a "habit" of drinking rather more than was exactly good for him." During this particular case, he is "out of temper" because of a newspaper article he is reading which questions his judicial abilities. Fang's treatment of the kind and respectable Brownlow shows his insensibility to matters of correct legal procedures. He is nothing more than a bad-tempered and drunken abuser of the law.

It is at this man's mercy that Oliver finds himself. Already shaken and exhausted from his harrowing experience, the child is further intimidated by his surroundings. As he waits for the decision of the magistrate, he is "deadly pale; and the whole place seemed turning round and round." When he is questioned by Mr. Fang, he is unable to respond. An assisting officer supplies standard answers to the questions so the magistrate will not be additionally infuriated.

Once he is cleared of the charge against him, Oliver is left to the kind and capable care of Mr. Brownlow. It appears that chance has thrown Oliver and Mr. Brownlow together, just as chance enabled the bookstall owner to arrive in time to clear Oliver's name. However, the faint suggestion that Brownlow recognizes something in Oliver's face and spends some considerable time trying to recall the association, indicates more than just a passing interest on Brownlow's part. Because of the refined and gentle qualities of the man, Oliver is, for the first time, in store for something good and hopeful.

CHAPTER 12

Summary
Oliver is taken by Mr. Brownlow to his home in Pentonville, a pleasant and well-kept suburb of London. There, he is cared for during his illness by Mrs. Bedwin, Brownlow's elderly and kind housekeeper.

For many days Oliver remains unconscious and ravaged by fever. When he eventually awakens, he is confused by his new surroundings and unaware of how he got there. He is reassured by Mrs. Bedwin, "a motherly old lady" who is touched by Oliver's sweet and grateful nature. Later he is visited by the doctor, a gentleman "with a very large and loud-ticking gold watch in his hand," who is glad to see his patient recovering.

For the next few days, Oliver is carefully attended by Mrs. Bedwin. As he gains strength, she has him carried to her room downstairs. There he notices a portrait on the wall of a lady with "a beautiful, mild face." Regarding it with fascination and awe, he explains to Mrs. Bedwin that he is drawn to it because "the eyes look so sorrowful; and where I sit, they seem fixed on me." The old housekeeper is unable to identify whose portrait it is. She turns his chair around so the picture will not upset him further.

A while later, Mr. Brownlow comes to visit his recuperating young guest. When he sees how weak and wasted Oliver is from his illness, the gentleman is moved to tears of pity. Brownlow mistakenly calls Oliver "Tom White" because that was the name supplied by the officer in the magistrate's office when Oliver was to weak to answer for himself. For a moment, Brownlow suspects that Oliver may be telling a lie. Then his attention is diverted when he again notices the resemblance in Oliver to someone he has known in his past. Staring intently at Oliver and pointing to the portrait on the wall, he excitedly calls Mrs. Bedwin's attention to the striking resemblance. Oliver's face "was its living copy. The eyes, the head, the mouth; every feature was the same." Because of Brownlow's sudden exclamation of surprise and because of his weakened condition, Oliver faints.

Commentary

Following the crucial events of his experiences with Fagin and the Dodger, Oliver at last achieves some measure of safety and benevolence in Mr. Brownlow's household. Lovingly watched over by the kindly and motherly Mrs. Bedwin, he is kept comfortable, clean and well-fed. When she offers him some strong broth, Dickens points out that if the soup were served in the workhouse and properly diluted, it would "furnish an ample dinner . . . for three hundred and fifty paupers, at the lowest computation." For the first time in his young life, Oliver is receiving proper food and comforts and kindness from others.

The mystery surrounding Oliver's resemblance is heightened in this chapter by his fascination with the portrait of an unknown woman. He senses some connection to her and says, "It makes my heart beat . . . as if it was alive and wanted to speak to me, but couldn't." When Brownlow enters and makes the startling discovery that Oliver resembles the woman in the painting, Dickens is clearly signalling the importance of the link between Oliver and Brownlow.

CHAPTER 13

Summary

While Oliver is removed to relative safety at Mr. Brownlow's, the Dodger and Charley Bates return in a roundabout way to Fagin's quarters. As they climb the rickety stairs, Fagin's sharply-tuned ears detect that only two of his boys are returning.

The old Jew angrily confronts them about Oliver's absence. When they make no reply, he resorts to physical abuse. He grabs the Dodger by the collar and threatens to beat him. At the same time, Bates falls to his knees and sets up a loud wailing

noise. The Dodger struggles free from Fagin's hold an̶
long fork which he uses to fend the "merry old gentlem̶
Fagin then turns his wrath on Bates and throws a heavy p̶
pot at the howling young man.

Suddenly, they are interrupted by the arrival of Bill Sikes.
Powerfully built and about 35 years old, Sikes has a rough and
mean appearance. He is accompanied by a big, white dog that is
well scarred from many battles. Their presence in the room
intimidates Fagin into a reasonable state of mind. After Sikes
has a few drinks, the four men discuss what has happened to
Oliver.

After listening to the Dodger's account of the incident,
Fagin and Sikes agree that Oliver knows too much about their
occupations and that he must be found and prevented from
informing on them. None of them is, however, able to come up
with a solution to their problem since each of them is naturally
reluctant to go near a police station. They are all too well-
known in the neighbourhood.

The answer arrives with the appearance of Bet and Nancy.
After much discussion and argument, they agree that Nancy is
the sensible choice since she is fairly new to the neighborhood
and will not likely be recognized by the police.

Supplied with articles of disguise by Fagin, Nancy poses as
Oliver's worried older sister. She wears a clean white apron, a
straw bonnet and carries a little covered basket.

After rehearsing her speech, Nancy departs for the police
station. On her arrival there, she visits the cells where the
prisoners are kept but is unable to find Oliver. Approaching a
policeman in the office, she performs her carefully prepared
portrayal of Oliver's distressed sister. The kind old man
explains what happened in the magistrate's office that day, and
tells her that Oliver was taken away by a gentleman who lives in
Pentonville.

On her return to Fagin's room, Nancy discloses what she
has learned. Sikes leaves immediately with his dog. Fagin distributes money to his helpers with instructions to find Oliver and
to kidnap him.

After they depart on their mission, Fagin makes preparations to move to another location. He lines his clothing with the
valuables he keeps under the floor and speaks of his desire to
have Oliver kidnapped.

Commentary

This chapter provides a contrast to the serenity of the preceding chapter. While Oliver is recovering in the comfort of Mr. Brownlow's house, Fagin and his companions are fighting and worrying about their own safety. As Dickens shows the reader the urgency and desperation of the band of thieves, he creates an atmosphere of tension regarding Oliver's security.

The clever scheme to send Nancy to inquire after Oliver illustrates the wit and daring of the criminals. Oliver can hardly be safe in his new-found happiness when such evil minds are plotting against him.

At the beginning of this chapter, Dickens spends considerable time expounding on the prevalence of the law of self-preservation. The fact that the Dodger and Bates so carelessly abandon Oliver, supposedly one of their own kind, when he is most in need of their help, gives Dickens the opportunity for ridicule. He is highly critical of those people who place their own self-interest above the needs of others and forget "any considerations of heart or generous impulse and feeling."

CHAPTER 14

Summary

To Oliver's disappointment, the fascinating portrait of the lady has been removed from the wall of the housekeeper's room. Mrs. Bedwin explains that it has been taken down to avoid causing Oliver further stress during his recovery.

His days are now spent happily in Brownlow's comfortable house. "Everything was so quiet, and neat, and orderly; everybody was kind and gentle." To Oliver "it seemed like Heaven itself." When he has recovered enough to get dressed, Mr. Brownlow provides him with a new suit of clothes and a new cap. With much relief, Oliver gives his old clothes to one of the servants, telling her she can sell them and keep the money.

Oliver and Mrs. Bedwin spend much time together. To pass the time, she teaches him to play cribbage (a card game), which Oliver learns quickly. One day, Oliver is summoned to Brownlow's study. Oliver is impressed with the great number of books he sees in the gentleman's study. Brownlow kindly asks Oliver to repeat an account of his life and advises him to "speak the truth, and you shall not be friendless while I live."

Oliver, who is apprehensive at the serious tone of their discussion and fears that Brownlow is going to turn him out of the house, prepares to tell his life's story. At that moment, they are interrupted by the announcement of the arrival of Mr. Grimwig, a friend of Mr. Brownlow. Brownlow warns Oliver about the visitor's behavior, saying he is "a little rough in his manners."

Grimwig appears and turns out to be a very peculiar character. He is a stout old gentleman who is lame in one leg and who blames his affliction on carelessly discarded orange peels. His is a gruff and imposing personality and, even when he is in agreement with his friends, he is known to have a "strong appetite for contradiction." His comment of offering to "eat [his] head" if his opinion is incorrect is his well-known trademark. Sometimes he punctuates this wager with a solid thumping of his cane on the floor.

Brownlow postpones his interview with Oliver until the next morning and sends the boy to order tea. Grimwig makes use of this opportunity to try to destroy Brownlow's good opinion of the boy. He warns Brownlow that Oliver is "deceiving you, my good friend." Brownlow, however, has a depth of belief in the boy that even he finds unaccountable. He replies to Grimwig that he would "answer for that boy's truth with [his] life!"

Oliver returns to the study and joins the two gentlemen for tea and muffins. After the meal, Mrs. Bedwin brings in a parcel of books that has been delivered from the bookstall where Brownlow was robbed. Brownlow, knowing that the bookstall owner is a poor man, is anxious to pay his bill immediately and to return some books. The messenger, however, has gone. Oliver, who is "delighted to be of use," agrees to run the errand. Grimwig turns this eager offer into a trial of Oliver's honesty. Brownlow accepts the challenge and says Oliver will be back in twenty minutes. Grimwig, irritated by his friend's confidence, predicts:

> The boy has a new suit of clothes on his back, a set of valuable books under his arm, and a five-pound note in his pocket. He'll join his old friends the thieves, and laugh at you. If ever that boy returns to this house, sir, I'll eat my head.

The two men put a watch on the table and sit in silence. Even after it becomes too dark to see the face of the watch, they are still waiting for Oliver.

Commentary

The threat to Oliver's idyllic existence is ominously present in this chapter. The reader is already aware of the outside forces that are at work to destroy his new happiness. Now, there is the added complication of Mr. Grimwig. These two dangers combine to release Oliver from his place of safety and expose him to the dangers of the plotting thieves.

Grimwig is a minor character with his own set of Dickensian peculiarities. His presence and pessimistic outlook provide the vehicle to move the protagonist into the action of the streets. His grim convictions about Oliver's character pose a threat to Brownlow's implicit belief in the boy.

The suspense attached to the mysterious connection between Brownlow and Oliver is emphasized again. The old gentleman is unable to explain why he has such a keen interest in the boy's welfare and why he trusts him so unquestioningly. Added to this is the absence of the mysterious portrait.

The characterization of Oliver is developing. Already recognized to be sweet-natured and honest, he appears in this chapter as kind-hearted and clever. Instead of burning or discarding his old clothes, he gives them to a servant who is allowed to sell them and keep the money. When Mrs. Bedwin teaches him to play cribbage, he learns "as quickly as she could teach." In the presence of Mr. Brownlow and Mrs. Bedwin, he is unfailingly polite and obedient because of his gratitude for their kindness.

CHAPTER 15

Summary

In a shabby neighborhood tavern, Bill Sikes is alone with his white, battle-scarred dog. Because of Sikes' brooding and drinking, the two engage in an exchange of physical abuses until the dog escapes when Fagin arrives.

There is an uneasiness between these two men. Sikes is contemptuous of the dishonest old Jew and Fagin is fearful of Sikes' brute strength and temperament. Each mistrusts the other yet each is dependent on the other for his own safety from the law. As Sikes warns, "If I go, you go."

Fagin has come to give Sikes his share of the plunder he has melted down into coins. A younger Jew named Barney, who works in the tavern, brings them drinks and informs them that Nancy has arrived. Still dressed in the guise of Oliver's "sister," she sits at their table on Bill's request. She starts to discuss what she has learned of Oliver's whereabouts but is abruptly silenced by a look from Fagin. A short while later she departs, again on a signal from Fagin, and Sikes accompanies her.

Out on the street, nearby, Oliver is happily making his way to the bookstall. He makes a wrong turn into a side street where he is confronted by a young woman who puts her arms around him and exclaims loudly, "Oh, my dear brother!" It is Nancy, and her convincing performance attracts the attention of people on the street. She is joined by Sikes who takes up his part in the little drama. He grabs the package of books from Oliver and announces to the bystanders that he is saving the child from his evil ways.

Oliver, who is weak and surprised by the attack, is unable to defend himself or make an escape. He is hurried away from the scene by Nancy and Sikes, much to the approval of the self-satisfied crowd.

While the kidnapping is taking place, Mrs. Bedwin is lighting the lamps at home and anxiously waiting his return. In the darkened study, Brownlow and Grimwig persevere in their vigil.

Commentary

Oliver's deliverance into the hands of the thieves is achieved. The ruthless elements of chance and coincidence have arranged circumstances to make his kidnapping an easy feat. The unsuspecting boy is whisked away from his new life in full view of credulous witnesses.

These incidental bystanders afford Dickens another opportunity for attack on the phenomenon of crowd mentality. Uninformed of the truth of the situation, they are ready to believe what they see and hear. When Nancy tearfully explains how Oliver left his parents and joined a set of thieves and bad characters, the bystanders are quick to condemn his behavior. When Sikes administers a heavy blow on Oliver's head with the parcel of books, the crowd is in approval. Only Oliver's pitiful but truthful protests are overlooked. He is helpless against the forces working against him.

In the tension among the thieves at the tavern, Dickens is exposing the uneasy atmosphere of mistrust in which the criminals live continually. They daily face the anxiety of being apprehended by the police and being hanged for their crimes. They also must deal with the uncertainty of trusting each other. Far from being a life of adventure and ease, their existence is presented as oppressive and troubled.

With the insertion of a short paragraph at the end of the chapter, Dickens reminds the reader of the terrible irony in Oliver's predicament. While he is being abducted by the thieves, Mrs. Bedwin and Mr. Brownlow maintain their anxious vigil, unaware of how hopeless it is.

CHAPTER 16

Summary

Night has fallen as Sikes and Nancy lead Oliver through the dark and foggy streets. Sikes warns Oliver to cooperate and instructs the mean white dog to intervene if the boy does not.

As they move through the quiet streets, a tolling church bell rings out eight o'clock. Nancy finds this to be a mournful reminder of the thieves who will be hanged when the clock next strikes eight. She speaks of her pity for them but is curtly rebuked by Sikes for her sentimentality.

Finally, they arrive at a dilapidated old house in a filthy narrow street. To gain entrance they must use a series of signals which are answered by the Artful Dodger. Downstairs in a "low earthy-smelling room," they are met by Charley Bates and Fagin.

Oliver is frightened by the taunts and laughter of the thieves. Bates circles him, threatening him with a stick while the Dodger empties his pockets. The old Jew welcomes him back with facetious good humor.

An argument ensues when the Dodger retrieves the five-pound note from Oliver's pocket. Fagin and Sikes dispute their rights to the money. Sikes eventually claims it for himself and Nancy in exchange for their "share of the trouble."

When they discuss the distribution of the books Oliver was

carrying, the child pleads for their return to Mr. Brownlow. He goes down on his knees "at the Jew's feet . . . in perfect desperation." Bargaining with his own life, Oliver asks only that they send the books back so that the kind old gentleman and lady will not think he has stolen them. His begging provokes the thieves to more merriment. As a last resort, Oliver starts hollering out loud for help and bolts out of the room. As Fagin and the two boys rush after Oliver, Nancy hurriedly closes the door after them so Bull's-eye, Sikes' vicious dog, cannot pursue Oliver.

When Oliver is brought back, Fagin picks up "a jagged and knotted club" which he brings down on Oliver's shoulders. Nancy intervenes on his behalf again. She is becoming passionate in her anger and stands against Fagin and Sikes. She threatens to get them all hanged if that will stop their malicious cruelty. Her fury is obstinate and even Sikes' imposing threats cannot calm her. As she rushes at Fagin, she is caught by Sikes and faints in her arms.

Bates takes Oliver to an adjoining bedroom where he must relinquish his new clothes. In return, he is dressed in the tattered rags he had previously given away. They were purchased by another Jewish fence of Fagin's acquaintance and provided him with a clue to Oliver's whereabouts.

To the sound of Bates' hysterical laughter and Bet's attempts to revive Nancy, Oliver falls into a dejected sleep.

Commentary

Similar to hunted animals, Fagin and his comrades have gone into hiding in the lower quarters of a broken-down house adorned with a decaying "to let" sign. They are further protected by a complicated system of signals to announce the arrival of visitors. Their elaborate precautions illustrate their constant fearfulness.

The unrestrained delight that Oliver's tormentors take in having recaptured him is punctuated with displays of overt cruelty. Oliver is humiliated repeatedly in order to amuse them. Their brutality and heartlessness reaches its peak with the crushing blow Fagin bestows on his shoulders.

As if to emphasize their violence, Nancy reacts with outraged protest. This sympathetic and humane aspect of her nature is evident early in the chapter when they are walking through the dark streets. As she expresses her pity for the criminals who are soon to be executed, she is reprimanded by Sikes. Even after she stops talking about it, Oliver is aware of her "deadly white" face and her trembling hand.

Nancy's defense of Oliver is so vehement that she defies Sikes and his nasty dog when Oliver tries to escape. All she receives for her noble effort is to be "flung . . . to the farther end of the room" by the powerful Sikes. Undaunted by the danger to herself, she intercedes when Fagin beats Oliver. She grabs the club from his hand and throws it into the fire.

Sikes, aware of her rising hysteria, tries to calm her with curses and threats. Instead of being pacified, she launches into an impassioned speech, citing her grievances against the Jew for bringing her young life to its present state of disrepute:

> . . . the cold, wet, dirty streets are my home; and you're the wretch that drove me to them long ago, and that'll keep me there, day and night, day and night, till I die!"

She regrets her responsibility for returning Oliver to them and their abuse. She explains:

> He's a thief, a liar, a devil, all that's bad, from this night forth. Isn't that enough for the old wretch, without blows?

Sikes and Fagin treat her outburst as a "common occurrence incidental to business." They ascribe her attempts to be "humane and gen—teel" as behavior typical of a woman. Since they are without compassion, they do not understand or accept this emotion in others. Fagin admits reluctantly that "it's the worst of having to do with women . . . but they're clever, and we can't get on . . . without 'em."

Nancy provides the only humane contact that Oliver has in this brutal world of criminals. And this fact is ironic. Her sensitivity and benevolence are products of the same environment that now endangers Oliver. It is because of her pitiable and miserable life with Fagin that she can offer some compassion.

Oliver's terrible predicament is presented in such a way as to gain sympathy from the reader. He is one small, helpless child caught in evil circumstances. His pathetic plea for the return of the books shows how selfless he is and how his only concern is for the regard of Mr. Brownlow who will be disappointed in him.

CHAPTER 17

Summary

Dickens opens this chapter with a preamble about his intention to change the setting of the action from the city back to the place of Oliver's birth. He explains that such abrupt transitions are as common in real life as they are in any work of fiction.

Mr. Bumble, the parochial beadle, is in especially fine spirits as he makes his way to see Mrs. Mann. He wants to impress her with the fact that he has been chosen by the board to take a coach to London to appear in court for a settlement dispute over two workhouse paupers. While he is there, he asks to see young Dick, Oliver's friend, of whom Mrs. Mann is complaining.

The small, sickly child is brought in. Wearing the "scanty parish dress" and appearing pale and thin, his wasted body makes him resemble an old man. When Bumble insensitively inquires if there is anything the child wants, Dick slowly and falteringly requests to be able to leave a message for "poor Oliver" after his death.

Bumble is dismayed by the request. Angrily, he sends Dick away to be locked in the cellar. Then he announces his intention of letting the board deal with this issue. Bumble and Mrs. Mann agree that the "outdacious Oliver" has influenced all the workhouse paupers.

Early the next morning, Bumble makes his journey. In London, he disposes of his "evil-minded" paupers, and settles down to a good meal, a drink and the newspaper.

He is startled to read an advertisement offering a reward of five guineas for information about the disappearance and/or background of Oliver Twist. Bumble immediately sets off to Pentonville to collect the money.

When Bumble is announced in Mr. Brownlow's study, he finds the gentleman in the company of Mr. Grimwig. Brownlow is impatient for news of Oliver and Grimwig is scornful of Bumble's profession.

After a 20-minute recital on the imperfections of Oliver's past behavior, Bumble receives the reward money and leaves.

Brownlow is extremely distressed by this information about Oliver, much to Grimwig's satisfaction. Brownlow explains the circumstances to Mrs. Bedwin who refuses to believe any of it. His last word on the subject is to order that he never wants to hear Oliver's name mentioned in his house again.

Commentary

In an effort to explain the intricacies of his developing plot, Dickens points out the need for such seemingly "absurd" transitions as he makes in this chapter. He explains that "in all good murderous melodramas," it is the custom to "present the tragic and the comic scenes, in . . . regular alternation." And, it is no different in real life, according to Dickens. People often move abruptly from "well-spread boards to death-beds, and from mourning weeds to holiday garments."

This chapter, then, serves to shift the main action from Oliver's plight in London to the town of his birth. The reader is instantly alerted to the potential danger of seeing Mr. Bumble prepare for his trip to the same city where Oliver now lives.

Nothing has changed in the workhouse world. Bumble is as pompous and heartless as ever. He and Mrs. Mann keep up the same pretenses about their concern for the paupers. Children are still mistreated and dying at the hands of the parish officials. Young Dick is as frail and ill as he was when Oliver last saw him.

The significance of changing the locale back to the workhouse is revealed in the fact that Bumble is going to London. It is a great coincidence that the beadle should make his trip just as an advertisement regarding Oliver should appear in that city's newspaper.

Bumble's subsequent visit to Mr. Brownlow is important for several reasons. The testimony Bumble gives of Oliver is damaging to Brownlow's faith in the child. Except for the unfailing belief of Mrs. Bedwin, Oliver is now without a single friend in the outside world. His fate at the hands of his captors seems unchangeable. While Mr. Brownlow may appear too easily convinced by Bumble's account of Oliver, it must be remembered that his is a very trusting nature. The report that Bumble gives is clearly supported in Brownlow's mind by Grimwig's prediction and Oliver's absence.

CHAPTER 18

Summary

The next day, Fagin begins a campaign to train Oliver. He starts by delivering a lecture on the "sin of ingratitude." He reminds Oliver of how he was taken in and cared for on his arrival to the city. He tells him chilling stories of other lads who acted similarly and had to be turned over to the hangman.

Once he has frightened Oliver with the terrible possibilities, he leaves him alone for several days to think about his future. After a week of this solitude, Fagin leaves the door of the room open to give Oliver the run of the rest of the dirty and neglected house. His only companions are spiders and mice. He becomes so lonely for human contact that he crouches for hours by the street door just to hear the sounds of people passing by.

One afternoon, the Dodger and Bates are in the house. The Dodger allows Oliver the privilege of polishing his boots. Oliver is thankful to have the company. Bates and the Dodger try to convince Oliver of the benefits of turning himself over to Fagin for training as a thief. Oliver is too timid and too clever to reveal his true opinion on the matter and says only, "I don't like it . . . I — I — would rather go." The Dodger and Bates persist in their arguments, saying that if Oliver doesn't steal there is someone else who will.

At this point, Fagin returns with Betsy and Tom Chitling, a man a few years older than the Dodger. The latter is shabbily dressed and explains that he has just been released from a six-week prison term.

Fagin and Chitling exchange a few words privately then the conversation is brought back to "the great advantages of the trade" for Oliver's benefit.

From this time on, Oliver is always included in the activities of the household. Sometimes they resume the "old game" with Fagin, and, at other times, Fagin amuses them with delightful stories of robberies he had committed in his younger days. Despite his natural reluctance, Oliver finds these tales humorous.

The period of Oliver's solitary confinement is over. Fagin's craftiness has tempered Oliver's young spirit into compliance:

Having prepared his mind, by solitude and gloom, to

prefer any society to the companionship of his own sad thoughts in such a dreary place, he was now slowly instilling into his soul the poison which he hoped would blacken it, and change its hue for ever.

Commentary

This chapter marks a very low point of Oliver's young life. Saddened by his enforced separation from Brownlow and tormented by the manipulations of Fagin, the future for Oliver looks very bleak. Alone and friendless, he is vulnerable to the influences around him.

Dickens makes it clear that Fagin is ruthless and clever. The entire program of persuasion that he uses on Oliver is effective. It is a system of psychological indoctrination, playing on the emotions of guilt, fear and loneliness. Oliver is young, inexperienced and impressionable. Fagin knows this and uses it to his advantage. By the time Oliver is allowed to be in the company of others, he has been deprived for so long that he is eager and receptive. This time-consuming investment on Fagin's part makes the reader aware that he has additional plans for Oliver.

CHAPTER 19

Summary

On a cold and misty night, Fagin dresses in heavy overclothes and sets out from his hiding place in Whitechapel. Winding his way through the familiar muddy streets and dark alleys, his destination is Bill Sikes' residence.

There, he is met by Sikes and Nancy. They offer him a drink, which he is reluctant to taste. To show him it is not poisoned, Sikes drinks it.

As they get down to business, Fagin speaks of the planned robbery of a house in Chertsey. It is Sikes' opinion that the job cannot be done. Toby Crackit, a specialist in his field of thievery, has been trying to bribe the servants of the house. His report that none of the servants will be corrupted makes their job almost impossible. Sikes and Fagin are discouraged.

After a long silence, Sikes reveals that he has an alternate plan, but he refuses to give the details because of his mistrust of Fagin. He will only say that he needs the services of a very small boy. At this point, Fagin tries to get Nancy out of the room in an effort to avoid another emotional display. Nancy, however, has already anticipated Fagin's suggestion of Oliver for the robbery. Sikes is hesitant but Nancy and the old Jew insist Oliver will be suitable.

They examine the advantages. Once Oliver is guilty of a robbery, he will have no way out of a criminal lifestyle. That will eliminate the possibility of his trying to make another escape. For Fagin, this is preferable to having Oliver put "out of the way." Fagin recognizes the value of Oliver's naïve appearance and vulnerability. Oliver can be "properly managed," more so than many other street paupers.

They agree on the use of Oliver and schedule the robbery for two nights later. Nancy will bring Oliver to Sikes who will be solely responsible for Oliver's cooperation. Once the plans are concluded, Sikes drinks himself into unconsciousness and Fagin leaves. When he arrives home, Fagin intends to tell Oliver of the plans but the boy is asleep. Fagin realizes how exhausted Oliver is and decides to wait until morning.

Commentary

A helpful coincidence arises for Fagin when Sikes needs a small boy like Oliver for his robbery. It provides Fagin with the opportunity to immerse the boy so thoroughly in a life of crime that he will never be able to get himself out. This latest ruse by the crafty old man illustrates to the reader how the clutches of evil are closing in on Oliver at a rapid pace.

The portrayal of Fagin in this chapter is a chilling one. Appearing like "some loathsome reptile," he glides and crawls through the "slime and darkness" of the streets. His familiarity with the area reveals how much a product of this squalid environment he is. Sikes calls him "the devil" and says he has the appearance of "a ugly ghost just rose from the grave." When the Jew grasps Sikes' hand during their discussion, Sikes pushes the hand away with disdain. The old man is a vile creature who stirs revulsion in those around him.

Nancy's eager suggestion to involve Oliver in the robbery effectively puts an end to any hope that the boy may have an ally on the inside. Her previous passionate defense of Oliver was based on her reluctance to see him physically abused. It seems natural to her now to have Oliver introduced into the kind of life that she lives.

Dickens also illustrates in this chapter how the thieves go about planning the considerable task of robbing a house. The job requires much preparation and attention to detail. An associate of Sikes' has been checking the house and laying the groundwork for the robbery. (His name, Crackit, is a humorous indication of his profession.) It is a dangerous and complicated business that they wish to involve Oliver in.

CHAPTER 20

Summary

The next morning, Oliver wakens to find that he has been provided with a new pair of sturdy shoes. At breakfast, Fagin informs him of the plans to send him to Bill Sikes, but does not disclose the details. Oliver, already accustomed to the unpredictable events of this lifestyle, expresses little curiosity about the venture. Fagin is disappointed in Oliver's lack of interest and the old man remains silent and uncommunicative until nightfall when he gets ready to go out.

Before the old man leaves, he gives Oliver a candle and a book to read while he waits for Nancy. Then, abruptly, Fagin solemnly warns Oliver to beware of Sikes who is "a rough man and thinks nothing of blood when his own is up."

After the old Jew is gone, Oliver leafs through the book which contains a detailed account of the lives of well-known criminals. He is horrified by the stories and falls on his knees to God to ask to be spared from such an infamous life.

Nancy arrives to convey Oliver to Sikes. She is pale and nervous and clearly uncomfortable about having to involve Oliver in the robbery. It occurs to Oliver, who senses her feelings, to appeal to her for help. She, in turn, is aware of his thoughts and pleads for his cooperation saying, "I have promised for your being quiet and silent; if you are not, you will only do harm to yourself and me too, and perhaps be my death." To verify her fear, she shows him bruises on her arms.

Nancy takes him by the hand and leads him outside to a waiting buggy that whisks them through the streets to Bill Sikes. All the while, Nancy implores him with "warnings and assurances" about his behavior. For a moment, when they arrive at Sikes' house, Oliver is tempted to cry for help but does not because of her "agony."

Inside, Sikes is waiting. He sits Oliver down and explains carefully the parts and workings of a pistol. As he holds the barrel of the gun to Oliver's head, he makes it clear that he would not hesitate to shoot the boy if Oliver makes a sound when they are out. To emphasize the threat, Nancy explains in plain language what Sikes means.

Sikes and Oliver sleep while Nancy sits brooding over the fire. Before daybreak the next morning, Oliver is awakened to get ready. As he and Sikes are about to leave, Oliver looks to Nancy for some encouragement but she avoids him and sits staring into the fire.

Commentary

Nancy's obvious agitation in her mission reveals the depth of her compassion for Oliver. She understands the child's fears and is reluctant to be involved in his corruption. It is evident from her explanations that she has already interceded on his behalf and has been physically punished for her efforts.

Nancy is caught in the throes of a moral dilemma. She is resigned to her own life of crime and accepts its burdens. At the same time, however, she is clearly disturbed by her part in the destruction of the child. When she tells Oliver "If I could help you, I would; but I have not the power," she is attesting to her own weakness and inability to overcome the evil influences in her life. When Sikes and Oliver leave in the morning, she is unable to meet Oliver's hopeful and pleading look.

Oliver's moral innocence is verified several times in this chapter. When Fagin tells him he will be going to Bill Sikes, Oliver naturally assumes he will be sent to "perform some ordinary menial offices for the housebreaker." When Fagin displays his contempt for Oliver's lack of interest in the venture, it is clear to the reader that the old Jew's training program has not completely corrupted Oliver. Later, as Oliver reads the book left by Fagin, his revulsion is so intense that he prays to die before allowing himself to "be reserved for crimes, so fearful and appalling."

The brutality of Sikes is reinforced here. He beats Nancy for intervening on Oliver's behalf and leaves her with "livid bruises" on her body. When Oliver arrives, Sikes puts the gun to the terrified boy's head and speaks threateningly. The reader knows that Sikes would carry out his threats with little or no provocation.

CHAPTER 21

Summary

It is a damp and gloomy morning when Sikes and Oliver set out. For the first part of their journey, the shops and streets are silent in the early morning hours. Later, Oliver is fascinated with the bustling activity of the awakening city.

Sikes drags Oliver along and they hurry through London. Near the Kensington area, they catch a ride on a cart. Passing through a succession of suburbs, Oliver is confused and wondering about their destination. All the while, he is conscious of Sikes' hand which clasps the pistol in the pocket of his coat.

At an inn called the Coach and Horses, Sikes and Oliver climb out of the cart and proceed again on foot. They eventually arrive in Hampton where they spend several hours walking in the fields outside of town. At suppertime, they enter the town and order dinner in an old public-house.

Oliver falls asleep after supper. When Sikes awakens him, it is a cold and misty night. Sikes asks one of the tavern's customers to give them a ride on his cart. After a few miles, they set out on foot and eventually come to a river past Shepperton. Oliver is frightened and assumes that Sikes means to murder him and dispose of his body in the river. Just as he is about to plead with Sikes, they arrive at a "ruinous and decayed" house which looks deserted. Taking Oliver's hand, Sikes leads him inside.

Commentary

It is a journey of some distance that Sikes and Oliver must make to reach their destination. Their itinerary across the city and through the western suburbs affords Dickens the opportunity of using his talent for descriptive details. He captures the activity of a great city coming to life in the morning. The movements of the people, the sights and the smells combine to create "a stunning and bewildering scene" of English life in Dickens' London.

This chapter serves as a transition to convey Sikes and Oliver to the scene of the upcoming burglary. The detailed length of their journey and Oliver's evident confusion add to the tension connected with Oliver's involvement in the crime.

CHAPTER 22

Summary

When Sikes and Oliver enter the dark house, they are met by Barney, the young Jew who is a waiter at the Three Cripples, and Toby Crackit, who is gaudily dressed in colorful clothes. The older men eat and drink heartily and force Oliver to swallow a half-glass of wine. Then they settle themselves for a nap before they go to work. Between the exhaustion from their journey and the glass of wine, Oliver, too, falls into a restless sleep.

At half past one in the morning, the men get up and start to prepare themselves and to gather the tools of their trade. Oliver watches them without comprehension.

Sikes and Toby place Oliver between them and go out into the cold night. They hurry through the empty streets and finally arrive at a house surrounded by a wall. The two robbers scale the wall with ease, lifting Oliver over with them. They silently approach the house.

As realization dawns on Oliver, he is "well-nigh mad with grief and terror." He breaks the silence and cries for mercy from Sikes: "let me run away and die in the fields . . . do not make me steal." Sikes is enraged and cocks the pistol but Toby intervenes with some quiet threats of his own.

Sikes proceeds with the work and expertly removes the shutters from a window at the back of the house. He instructs Oliver to go through the hall and open the street door for them. Then Sikes hoists him through the window.

Once inside, Oliver makes up his mind to inform the occupants of the house of the burglary. Just as he moves from the window, he hears Sikes calling after him to come back. Oliver freezes, not knowing what to do. Suddenly, two men appear at the top of the stairs and fire a pistol. Sikes grabs Oliver and fires his own gun. They retreat through the window.

A great deal of noise commences as the thieves make their getaway. Sikes carries Oliver who has been wounded. As they run away from the house, Oliver slips into unconsciousness.

Commentary

Oliver's naïve assumptions regarding their destination continue until they reach the house where the burglary is to take place. Once he becomes aware of the men's intention, he is horrified and begs to be released. He would rather die in the fields than be an accomplice in the crime. When he is placed inside the house, he is even willing to risk his life to warn the residents. Despite the time he has spent with Fagin and the thieves, he is no more inclined to this lifestyle than he was when Brownlow was robbed.

When Oliver is discovered in the house and wounded by a gunshot, the reader is reminded of Nancy's hesitation in previous chapters to subject Oliver to a life of crime. The reasons are now evident. This is a mortally dangerous business that Oliver has been forced to participate in.

It is worth noting that the activities of the thieves are always associated with darkness, fog and gloom. Fagin and Sikes both prefer to move about through the streets under the protective cover of night. For this burglary too, the thieves hide their movements in the "silence of the night." This is clearly done for practical reasons but Dickens makes it clear that what they do is not fit to be seen in sunlight. They are evil characters who function in suitable darkness.

CHAPTER 23

Summary

The chapter opens on a bitterly cold night. In the workhouse where Oliver was born, Mrs. Corney, the matron, is making tea.

As she works, she contemplates her good fortune. She considers the workhouse paupers, who do not seem as grateful as she for what they have. When she accidently spills hot water on her hand, her mood changes and she begins to lament her "solitary fate" and the death of her husband 25 years earlier.

At this point, she is interrupted by the entrance of Mr. Bumble. They speak of the cold weather and then discuss the ingratitude of the paupers. They agree that no matter how hard the parish tries to alleviate the suffering of the poor people, the paupers are not contented. Bumble tells her stories to support his opinion and then confides in her about "the great principle" of the parish workhouse. He explains that the official premise of this principle is to "give the paupers exactly what they don't want; and then they get tired of coming."

When Bumble is about to leave, Mrs. Corney invites him to tea. He accepts and they sit at a table in front of the fire. As they speak, Bumble begins to make romantic advances towards his hostess and then kisses her. They are interrupted by a knock at the door. Mrs. Corney is requested to attend to Old Sally, a dying pauper. Indignant at the interruption, Mrs. Corney agrees to go but first requests Mr. Bumble to wait for her. While she is gone, Bumble inspects the contents of her room.

Commentary

In this comic chapter the attitudes of Mrs. Corney and Mr. Bumble are highlighted. They both consider the paupers are ungrateful for what they receive, which we know is actually very little. Bumble confesses this giving of little is the official parish principle.

Mrs. Corney is shown as a hard, unkind woman annoyed at having her meals and courtship interrupted by dying paupers. Bumble is shown as greedy and selfish in his pursuit of Mrs. Corney.

CHAPTER 24

Summary

Mrs. Corney is led by the old woman to a bare attic room. There, the dying woman lies unconscious on the bed, attended by another old pauper and the apprentice of the apothecary.

Mrs. Corney and the apprentice speak of the weather until he takes his leave. Mrs. Corney, who is impatient and aware of the waiting Mr. Bumble, is about to do the same when the dying woman sits up in bed. Old Sally orders her two attendants out of the room so she can speak in private to the matron.

As Mrs. Corney listens with disinterest, Old Sally tells her story. Years ago in this same room, she nursed a young woman who gave birth to a child and died. Before her death, though, she told Old Sally of a valuable gold object she had which she wanted to be given to her child. Old Sally now confesses that she stole this object after the woman died.

Mrs. Corney listens eagerly now as Old Sally goes on. She says "They *called* him Oliver. . . . The gold I stole was —." Then she falls back on the bed and the secret dies with her. Mrs. Corney leaves the room and informs the two old women that Old Sally had "nothing to tell, after all."

Commentary

The callous attitude towards the everyday event of death in the workhouse is illustrated in this chapter. The apothecary's apprentice is bored with his attendance in the sick room. Mrs. Corney is annoyed at having been called away from her pleasant room and Mr. Bumble. The two old paupers are not distressed by the loss of one of their friends but are rather enjoying the diversion.

The dying woman is not an incidental occurrence used simply to evoke sympathy in the reader. She is the old pauper who attended Oliver's mother the night he was born. When she speaks of a mysterious gold object and of the young mother's concern that her child "would not feel so much disgraced to hear its poor young mother named," the suspense regarding Oliver's past is increased dramatically. The only person with any knowledge of his mother now lies dead with her important secret.

Dickens uses these last two chapters to divert the reader's attention from the critical point in the main action. At the end of Chapter 22, Oliver has been wounded by a gunshot. Now the author prolongs the suspense of Oliver's condition and further complicates the plot with the addition of these workhouse chapters. The mystery surrounding Oliver's origin has deepened.

CHAPTER 25

Summary

While Old Sally is telling her tale to Mrs. Corney, Fagin sits in his room brooding over the fire. Near him, at a table playing cards, are the Dodger, Charley Bates and Tom Chitling. The Dodger is cheating by looking at Tom's cards. Finally, after the Dodger wins a number of games, Tom becomes upset and they stop playing.

The boys take to teasing Tom about his affection for Betsy. Tom admits that he went to prison to protect her, but he is also proud of the fact that he did not turn her in. Bates finds cause for much laughter in Tom's story until Tom responds with anger and attacks him. Bates avoids the blow which lands instead on Fagin's chest.

At that moment, the bell rings and the Dodger goes to investigate. He returns and talks privately to Fagin who reacts with surprise. The Dodger goes out again and the old man sends Bates and Chitling out of the room. The Dodger brings in Toby Crackit who looks tired and worn.

Even though Fagin is impatient to hear what news Toby brings, the visitor asks for food and drink, claiming he has not eaten for three days. He eats at a leisurely pace while Fagin watches in exasperation. When Toby is finished, he orders the Dodger out of the room.

Toby's first remark is to ask after Bill Sikes. Fagin, who already knows from the newspapers about the failed robbery, is astounded that Toby does not know of Bill or Oliver's whereabouts.

Toby explains what happened that night, adding that when they were carrying Oliver away from the house, they were pursued by men and dogs. To speed their getaway, they left Oliver in a ditch. In Toby's words, it was a case of "every man for himself, and each from the gallows!" The report causes Fagin to run from the house in a rage.

Commentary

The return of Toby Crackit to Fagin's house is an ominous sign that causes the reader to wonder about Oliver. Even with Toby's account of their escape at the end of this chapter, there is no further information regarding the boy and his bullet wound.

The fact that Sikes and Toby abandoned Oliver and adhered to the principle of "every man for himself," belies Tom Chitling's earlier remark about serving time in prison rather than turning in Betsy. The code of honor that exists among the criminals is seen to be easily adaptable to suit the circumstances.

When this chapter opens, Fagin is brooding and lost in deep thought. He is oblivious to the playful antics of the boys. At the end of the chapter, it is revealed that at least three days have passed since the attempted robbery. Clearly, Fagin has been worried about Oliver's return. When he hears Toby's story, he is unable to control himself further and leaves the house in a fury of temper.

CHAPTER 26

Summary

Walking through the streets in a "wild and disordered

manner," Fagin makes his way towards Saffron Hill and the tavern called the Three Cripples. The neighborhood is the domain of many of the criminals in the city who nod agreeably to Fagin as he passes by. At one of the stalls, he stops to ask a dealer of stolen goods, Mr. Lively, about Bill Sikes. Unable to gain any information, he hurries on to the tavern.

There he closely inspects the faces of the customers, looking for someone in particular. He signals to the landlord of the establishment and they step outside the room to talk. The man confirms to Fagin that he has had no word from Barney, the waiter from the tavern who was with Sikes and Toby. Then Fagin inquires about a man named Monks who, he is told, will be arriving soon. Fagin, however, is reluctant to wait for Monks and heads home.

Fagin stops on his way at Sikes' residence. Nancy is alone there and in a state of deep depression over the missing Sikes. She is incoherent and can offer Fagin no help. He turns the subject to Oliver, hoping to draw a more definite response from her. Her reaction is to comment vehemently that she hopes the boy is dead and out of harm's way.

Fagin becomes angry with her attitude and unleashes a flurry of threats on Sikes. He is infuriated at the thought of losing Oliver who represents a potentially large income. In his excitement, he begins to talk about being "bound to . . . a born devil," but he checks himself, trembling "with the apprehension of having himself disclosed some hidden villainy." He is fearful that he may have revealed too much to Nancy. He questions her slyly and is relieved to see that she is too affected by liquor to have understood his remarks. He leaves, satisfied that Sikes has not returned.

It is close to midnight as Fagin heads for home through the cold and windy streets. Near his house, he is confronted by a man hovering in the shadows. Fagin leads him into the house with obvious reluctance. He then checks on Crackit and the boys who are all safely asleep. He and the visitor move to an upstairs room to talk.

The man, who is Monks, and Fagin converse in whispers. Monks is "in a state of considerable irritation" and Fagin appears to be "defending himself against some remarks." Finally, Monks raises his voice and expresses his opinion that "it was badly planned." He demands to know why Fagin didn't keep "him" here among the rest. Monks suggests that the old man might have "got him convicted" and safely sent away. Fagin protests, explaining how difficult a pupil the boy was. Now, if he is dead, Fagin has lost his investment. And, if he is alive, Fagin has his own safety to worry about. Monks declares fervently that he had nothing to do with the boy's death if that is the case. Suddenly Monks utters a startled exclamation and tells Fagin that he saw the shadow of a woman pass by on the wall. Fagin leads him through the house to convince him that they are alone. Finally, Monks admits it must have been his imagination. He laughs uncomfortably and leaves.

Commentary

The atmosphere in this chapter is charged with danger and mystery. Fagin is preoccupied and visibly agitated. His conversation with the landlord at the Cripples is vague and suspicious. The fact that he is looking for a man that he really does not want to see is curious. In his interview with Nancy he is distracted with worry and anger and almost blurts out secret information. The midnight meeting with Monks adds to the perplexity of the situation.

It is interesting that Dickens adds the character of Monks at this point in the novel. He is a sinister man whose sudden appearance brings out further surprising information. He clearly is playing a significant part in the activities that have taken place. From his conversation with Fagin, it is evident that he knew of Sikes' planned robbery and of its subsequent failure. He seems also to be aware of Fagin's interest in Oliver. The "boy" that they are discussing is clearly Oliver and they are not in agreement about him. Fagin is on the defensive against this man who seems to have some power over the old Jew.

Monks is a mysterious character in this chapter. No description of him is provided for the reader. He is more of a presence, a "dark figure" who glides out from the shadows in the street, a mere voice talking in a whisper. Yet, his strange power is felt because of Fagin's obvious fear of him. When they are discussing Oliver's possible death, Monks makes it clear that he had nothing to do with it. He may be a criminal but he is opposed to murder. In his own defense, he says:

I won't shed blood; it's always found out, and haunts

a man besides. If they shot him dead, I was not the cause. . . .

The mysterious "shadow of a woman" that Monks sees while they are talking adds to the sinister atmosphere and tension of the action. Monks is uneasy and leaves soon after this.

Clearly, the events of this chapter combine to present a baffling puzzle of mystery and suspense.

CHAPTER 27

Summary
The action returns to the workhouse where Mr. Bumble is still awaiting the return of Mrs. Corney. Since she is gone some time, he contents himself with counting and re-counting her possessions. He even checks through her dresser drawers and is pleased to find a cash box.

When she comes in, she is flustered and breathless from her interview with Old Sally. As she recovers herself with the help of some "medicine" from a glass bottle, Mr. Bumble continues his courtship. He tells her frankly that he admires her material comforts and suggests that they are enough for two. He hints at the approaching death of Mr. Slout, the workhouse master, and makes it clear that he regards himself as a suitable replacement. Finally, Mrs. Corney is convinced and agrees happily to marry him. She tells him that she will reveal more details of Old Sally's death after they are married. They exchange another long and affectionate embrace. Bumble leaves to notify the undertaker of Old Sally's death.

At Sowerberry's establishment, only Noah Claypole and Charlotte are at home. Bumble watches through the window as the two servants enjoy a feast of oysters. When Noah asks Charlotte for a kiss, Bumble enters and reprimands them severely. The outraged beadle gives Noah orders regarding a coffin for Old Sally for the next day. He leaves, full of indignation at the wickedness of the lower orders.

Commentary
Dickens speaks directly to the reader again in this chapter in order to explain yet another digression from the main action. Because of the apparent virtue and prestige of parochial beadles

like Bumble, Dickens says it would be unsuitable to leave "so mighty a personage . . . waiting." At the same time, the author uses this opportunity to reveal more of the disagreeable qualities of the beadle's character.

Bumble has been quite content during his wait. He has examined every possession and piece of furniture in the matron's room a "full half a dozen times." Because of the satisfactory number of possessions, he decides she will be a suitable wife for him. His tender feelings for the matron are motivated by greed.

As the courtship progresses, both Bumble and Mrs. Corney are made to appear humorous. They are very alike and do seem well-matched. Both are selfish and materially oriented. Both despise the paupers in whose midst they work. Their attraction for each other is based on comforts and greed.

The mystery of Old Sally's last words to Mrs. Corney remains undisclosed. The old matron is reluctant to speak of them until after she and Bumble are married. It is natural to assume that, since a valuable gold object was mentioned, Mrs. Corney is not willing to share the knowledge of it.

The incident at the undertaker's affords Dickens the chance to illustrate Bumble's great hypocrisy. He has just left the arms of his future bride but is angered and appalled to find Noah and Charlotte engaging in similar activity. The fact that he is spying on them through a window escapes his attention. He directs his moral outrage at their "sin and wickedness" which is actually no worse than his own.

At the end of the chapter, Dickens announces that the story is returning to the plight of Oliver who was left so unmercifully in a ditch at the end of Chapter 22.

CHAPTER 28

Summary
This chapter resumes the action with the hasty flight of the thieves from the scene of the robbery. Sikes is burdened with the weight of the unconscious Oliver. He stops to rest and calls after the fleeing Crackit. It is Toby who suggests leaving the child behind and it takes Sikes only moments to agree with this course of action. He leaves Oliver on the ground, covered with a cape.

The group of pursuers is made up of Mr. Giles, a butler in

the house where the robbery was attempted, Brittles, a general handyman, a traveling tinker and two dogs. They stop their manhunt by agreement because, as one man says, they are "all afraid."

Meanwhile, as day breaks cold and wet, Oliver regains consciousness. Weak from loss of blood and in considerable pain, Oliver gets to his feet and staggers off for help. His thoughts are confused and he doesn't know where he is. Eventually, he comes to a house which he recognizes from the night before. With what strength he has left, he approaches the door, lightly knocks, and then falls into a heap on the porch.

Inside the house, Giles and Brittles are entertaining the other staff members with an exaggerated account of their bravery during the robbery. When they hear a sound at the door, they are all too frightened to answer it. After much delay, they agree to open the door together.

They find Oliver helplessly crouched by the door. They drag him roughly into the house and triumphantly declare the capture of one of the thieves. The commotion attracts the attention of a young lady of the house. She comes downstairs to investigate. After consultation with her aunt, who is mistress of the house, the girl gently orders Giles to put the injured person in his own room and to go for the doctor and a policeman. The girl refuses to look at the captured thief but only asks Giles to treat him kindly.

Commentary

Dickens picks up the action on the night of the robbery so that the reader does not miss any developments in Oliver's predicament.

The author reveals the real fear of Sikes and Crackit as they abandon Oliver and run for their lives. The irony of the chase is that they are being pursued by an odd assortment of gentlemen who are equally afraid. These men call off the pursuit when they all admit to their fright. Later, when Giles the butler is telling the story, he conveniently adapts it to make himself and the other two men appear heroic in their attempts to apprehend the thieves. Their bravery, however, is put to the test again when they hear a sound at the door. Their fear returns and they are too cowardly to investigate.

Their triumph and self-satisfaction at Oliver's "capture"

renders them even more ridiculous. They are grown men delighting in their own sense of importance while Oliver lies pathetically at their feet.

Now that the action has returned to Oliver, the reader can see just how precarious his fate is at this moment. Sick and confused by his injury, he inadvertently places himself in the hands of the people Sikes was trying to rob. The pompous heroism of Giles and Brittles places him in further danger because they only wish to see him survive so that he may be hanged for his crime.

There is one suggestion of hope and comfort for Oliver in the presence of the young lady who speaks in a sweet and gentle voice. She appears genuinely concerned for the welfare of the injured thief even though she is not yet aware that he is a mere child. On her aunt's kind orders, Oliver is conveyed carefully to a bedroom while a doctor is sent for.

CHAPTER 29

Summary
Mrs. Maylie, the mistress of the house, and her niece, Rose, are having breakfast served by a smartly dressed Giles. They are waiting for the arrival of the doctor and comment anxiously on how long it seems to be taking Brittles on his errand.

Soon after this, Mr. Losberne, the neighborhood doctor, arrives in a carriage. After a pleasant exchange with the ladies, he attends to the patient in the upstairs bedroom.

The doctor is absent for a long time and there is a great deal of activity in the household while the servants dash about to help the surgeon. When he finally returns to the ladies, he persuades them that they should visit the patient. Giles has neglected to mention that the culprit of the crime is only a young boy. The doctor does not tell them this but only insists there is no danger to them.

Commentary
Despite the physical discomfort of his injuries, Oliver is in a protected and comfortable environment once again. The ladies of the house are described in terms that make them appear kindly and good. The aunt is a well-dressed, stately woman and her niece is gentle and beautiful. Even the fat doctor who comes

to treat Oliver is kind and hearty. The comfortable home and pleasant furnishings combine with the aspects of these characters to create a dramatic contrast to Oliver's recent associations in the sinister world of the thieves.

The fact that Giles has not yet informed his mistress of the age of the thief attests to his cowardice. He wanted to prolong his moment of glory as the brave defender of the house for a while longer. The reader can predict what the reactions of the two gentle ladies will be when they discover who the criminal is.

CHAPTER 30

Summary

Mr. Losberne makes a great and ironic ceremony out of leading the ladies upstairs to inspect the criminal. They have preconceived impressions of finding a "dogged, black-visaged ruffian" and are naturally astonished to see, instead, a small child worn with pain and exhaustion.

Rose is moved to tears of compassion for the boy and Mrs. Maylie is incredulous. Rose pleads with her aunt to have mercy on the boy. The aunt assures her that she will do whatever she can to protect him.

Mrs. Maylie turns to the doctor for advice. After much thought, he proposes to interview the boy when he wakes to ascertain if he is "a real and thorough bad one." If he is, the doctor will not do any more to help him. In the meantime, he is going to interrogate Giles and Brittles to try and gain their cooperation.

The three of them wait for Oliver to awake. It is evening when he does and they listen to the heartbreaking account of his life. The listeners are all moved to tears of sympathy.

Later, in the kitchen, Mr. Losberne confronts the servants and a local constable. The doctor challenges Giles and Brittles to make a positive identification of Oliver as the same lad they encountered during the robbery. They are bewildered and hesitant to answer. At that moment, runners from the Bow Street police station arrive at the house. The doctor is annoyed at the interruption.

Commentary

Again, Oliver experiences a dramatic reversal of his fate.

Torn away from the haven of Mr. Brownlow's house, he is sub-
jected to the evil manipulations of the thieves. His well-being
then reaches a crucial point when he is wounded during the
robbery. Now, at last, he appears to be safely surrounded by
comfort and benevolence.

Oliver's goodness and morality are being rewarded here.
His unfailing attempts to live honestly and away from evil
influences are qualities that affect the kind hearts of Mrs.
Maylie and her niece. Even the initially skeptical Mr. Losberne
is moved to tears when he hears Oliver's life story.

The fact that Mr. Losberne is willing to put his professional
reputation on the line by swaying the testimony of the servants
is proof of the extent of the houschold's desire to help Oliver.

CHAPTER 31

Summary

Brittles is still uneasy when he goes to the door to admit the
officers. Blathers, a stout man of about 50, is in charge and
Duff is his "bony" and "red-headed" companion.

Mr. Losberne introduces the ladies of the house and launches into a lengthy account of the burglary in order to buy time
for Oliver. When Blathers inquires about "this here boy," the
doctor tries to make light of the matter and to dismiss the
notion of the boy's involvement. To distract the officers further, Losberne offers to show them the window where the
robbers attempted to make their entry.

Blathers and Duff make a thorough inspection of the
premises. Then they interrogate Giles and Brittles. The two servants are confused and uncertain about their replies and continually contradict each other's story.

While the officers confer in private, the doctor expresses
his concern for Oliver. He does not think the policemen will be
convinced by the boy's account of his involvement. As the
ladies implore him for a solution, he decides they must come up
with a bold plan.

The policemen return with the conclusion that it was not a
"put-up robbery," one in which the servants were bribed by the
burglars. They decide it was the work of criminals from the city
because "the style . . . is first-rate." They also deduce that the
work was done by two men and a boy.

When Blathers again refers to the wounded boy, the doctor tries to forestall that interrogation by offering the men a drink.

Warmed by the liquor and encouraged by Rose's eagerness to engage them in conversation, the officers relate the strange incidents of another crime they once handled. In that story, Conkey Chickweed was robbed of his money and reported wounding a mysterious tall man with a black patch over his eye. Investigations by the Bow Street officers failed to turn up any clues. After several unsuccessful attempts to pursue the elusive criminal with the black patch, the officer in charge, a Jem Spyers, concluded that Chickweed had robbed himself.

Losberne, who has slipped away and returned during the story, now invites the officers upstairs to see the boy. In the bedroom, Oliver appears to be feeling worse than ever. He is more feverish and unable to comprehend what is going on around him. Mr. Losberne defiantly delivers a concocted story of how the boy was accidentally injured by a gunshot on the neighbor's premises. When the child came to the Maylie house for help, he was mistakenly identified as one of the robbers.

Blathers asks the "bewildered butler" to verify this story. Giles stammeringly agrees to it and then admits he cannot swear to recognizing the boy as the culprit. When Brittles is called in, his confused account is similar to Giles'.

The police officers next examine the gun that the butler supposedly used but which is actually one of a matched pair. They find that it is loaded only with gunpowder and brown paper, because the good doctor had secretly removed the bullet. Giles is relieved to think that he is not, after all, responsible for wounding the poor boy upstairs.

Blathers and Duff retire to Chertsey for the night with the promise that they will return the next day. Their visit is canceled when the investigators journey instead to a prison where three suspects are being held. The two men and a boy were arrested for sleeping under a haystack. They turn out not to be the culprits in question.

Mrs. Maylie and the doctor post a bond with a local magistrate for Oliver's appearance "if he should ever be called upon." Blathers and Duff are rewarded with some money and they return to London. Their final analysis is that "the burglarious attempt had originated with the Family Pet" or with "Mr. Conkey Chickweed."

70

Oliver is safe from the police. Under the loving care of the household, his recovery progresses.

Commentary

Dickens' skillful and humorous presentation of the incompetent Bow Street officers renders Losberne's deceit of them more harmless. They are comical and inept in their duties and their portrayal is intended to illustrate Dickens' opinion of the inadequacies of the law enforcement system.

Losberne is a respectable citizen and professional who risks his own integrity to defend Oliver, whom he believes is an innocent victim. He is intelligent enough to realize that the inferior abilities of the officers will prevent them from having this faith in their fellow man. They will want the facts of Oliver's story and Losberne recognizes that the facts can be misinterpreted. Dickens is again expressing his belief in humanity that is based on accepting the benevolence in people. It is Dickens' opinion that justice is arbitrary and that mercy and charity are better institutions to adhere to.

Owing to the overall kindness in the Maylie household and to the dogged efforts of Losberne, Oliver is delivered safely from the questionable hands of the law. His sordid past seems now to be behind him forever and he is free to bask in the warmth and affection of his new benefactors.

CHAPTER 32

Summary

For many weeks, Oliver endures the healing of his broken arm and the onset of fever and chills. Gradually, he gains his strength and promises to repay the kindness afforded to him by Mrs. Maylie and Rose. Rose assures him there will be plenty of time for his gratitude when they move to their summer home. His only concern during this period of recovery is for Mr. Brownlow and Mrs. Bedwin who would be pleased if they knew of his well-being.

When Oliver is strong enough, Losberne takes him by carriage to visit Mr. Brownlow. On the way, Oliver recognizes a house in Chertsey and excitedly informs the doctor that it is the same house from which the robbers operated.

Immediately, Losberne jumps from the carriage and

invades the house which is occupied by a hunchback. They engage in an argument and the doctor demands to know of Sikes. The cripple reacts defensively and denies any knowledge of the matter. Before he leaves, Losberne notices that the interior of the house in no way matches Oliver's description. Back in the carriage he regards Oliver with a sharp and fierce look that betrays his suspicious thoughts.

In Pentonville, they stop in front of the white house where Oliver had been so happy. The child is naturally astounded when they see a "To Let" sign in the window. They make inquiries of the neighbors and learn that Brownlow, Mrs. Bedwin and a third person moved to the West Indies six weeks ago.

Dejectedly, Oliver suggests a visit to the owner of the bookstall. He is the last possible source of support for Oliver's story. Losberne, however, makes a decision to return to Chertsey.

Oliver is disappointed at not having the opportunity to clear himself with the kind Mr. Brownlow. His sorrow is partially alleviated by the preparations they are making to go to the country. Within two weeks, they are ready to depart and leave the house in Giles' care.

It is springtime and the countryside is tranquil and beautiful. To Oliver, who has spent his entire life amid the squalid confines of the city and the workhouse, this country retreat is a powerful restorative. He and the Maylies spend peaceful days reading, walking in the gardens and in the village, and singing happy songs at the piano. Every morning, Oliver is tutored in reading and writing by a neighborhood gentleman. He is also learning about gardening from the village clerk. Whenever he can, he is eager to perform useful services for the ladies to repay their abundant kindness.

In this idyllic environment, Oliver spends three happy months with his benefactors.

Commentary

After the tumultuous events and tensions of several preceding chapters, this chapter provides a pleasant contrast. Freed from his evil associates, recovered from his injuries and attended lovingly by the two ladies, Oliver's life has been transformed.

Dickens attributes Oliver's return to well-being to more than just the kindly ministering of the Maylies. He describes in lush detail the beauty and serenity of the countryside setting. It is "a glimpse of Nature's face" that provides all people with an opportunity to refresh themselves. After the crowded streets and the "narrow boundaries" of city life, the country is an effective remedy.

The presence of gentility and many refined qualities associated with Mrs. Maylie and her country neighbors provides added contrast to Oliver's former lifestyle. Walks, reading, flowers and music make up the idyllic days for Oliver and his companions. Even the poor people of the village are neat and clean, as are the houses they visit on charity calls. In the churchyard, "humble mounds, covered with fresh turf" mark the resting places of the villagers. This is very different from the crowd of "tall unsightly gravestones" that Oliver has seen and where he imagines his poor mother is buried.

It should be noted that, in this novel, people who are educated and associated with books are made to appear of a better quality than those who are not. Mr. Brownlow with his study full of great books is Oliver's first introduction to a kind and more sophisticated world. Similarly with the Maylies, he finds himself surrounded by a kindness that seems to be the product of an experience with reading, music and the Bible.

CHAPTER 33

Summary
Summer arrives and the countryside blooms "into strong life and health" which matches Oliver's complete recovery. He grows into a stout and healthy lad but remains "the same gentle, attached, affectionate creature" that he has always been.

One beautiful evening, after Oliver and the ladies return from a stroll, Rose is very solemn and begins to cry uncontrollably. Mrs. Maylie is alarmed by the sudden alteration in the girl. Rose confesses that she does feel very ill and she goes to bed.

When they are alone, Oliver and Mrs. Maylie express their fears about Rose's health. Mrs. Maylie is gravely concerned and Oliver tries to comfort her by saying "Heaven will never let her die so young." Mrs. Maylie speaks with the experience of her years and gently tells the boy "that it is not always the youngest and best who are spared to those that love them."

When morning comes, Rose is dangerously ill with a fever. Mrs. Maylie sends Oliver to the village with a message for Mr. Losberne. She hesitates and decides not to send another letter that is addressed to "Harry Maylie, Esquire."

Oliver leaves and runs the four miles with "the greatest speed he could muster." At a tavern called The George, the landlord arranges a special messenger to take the letter on horseback.

As Oliver hurries to return home, he collides with a strange, tall man who utters snarls and curses at the boy. As Oliver watches, the man falls on the ground in a convulsion. Before he leaves, Oliver arranges to get help from the tavern for the stranger.

That day, Rose's condition becomes progressively worse. A local doctor is summoned. His outlook for her recovery is not very hopeful. The entire household is tense with grief and suspense over the girl's illness. The next morning, Mr. Losberne arrives and agrees that her condition is grave.

Another day passes in "agony and passion" for Oliver. Helplessly he walks about, uttering prayers and weeping. Sitting in the churchyard amid the peace and beauty of "the sunny landscape," he cannot believe that a fair young girl like Rose can die while all around nature is thriving. As he sits there, the church bell tolls for the funeral of some other young person.

In deep sorrow, Oliver heads homeward. He finds Mrs. Maylie keeping her steadfast vigil for the girl. She tells Oliver that Rose is in a deep sleep that will result in recovery or death. Many hours later, Losberne comes to tell them that Rose will live. The crisis has passed. Mrs. Maylie falls on her knees in thankfulness.

Commentary

The perfect serenity of life is disrupted in this chapter by Rose's critical illness. The crisis is a poignant reminder by the author that everyone is susceptible to danger and death. It is a startling paradox that youth can be stricken with death while nature persists in her beauty. In his innocence, Oliver cannot accept this fact of life until he is grimly reminded of its reality in the churchyard. He sees the procession of mourners for some young person who has died and he is amazed that "the sun shone brightly, and the birds sang on."

This new insight causes him to reflect on a common human misgiving. Dickens is of the opinion that we never fully appreciate what we have until it is too late. Oliver knows that he has been devoted to Rose for her goodness to him, but he still feels that there might have been something more he could have done to express his love and gratitude. And so it is with all of us. Dickens reminds us that:

> We need to be careful how we deal with those about us, when every death carries to some small circle of survivors, thoughts of so much omitted, and so little done — of so many things forgotten, and so many more which might have been repaired! There is no remorse so deep . . . .

Two other incidents in this chapter provide the reader with cause for anticipation. One is the mention of a Mr. Harry Maylie and the other is Oliver's encounter with the wild-looking man at the tavern. With the first, it is evident that Dickens is going to introduce a new character who is somehow connected to Rose and her aunt. With the second, there is a dangerous and foreboding feeling associated with the chance appearance of the strange man.

CHAPTER 34

Summary
Oliver is overcome with joy and gratitude at Rose's recovery. On a long walk, he finds consolation in tears. Heading home near nightfall, he meets a carriage that is racing to the Maylie house. Inside the coach are Giles, still in his nightcap, and Harry Maylie who is Mrs. Maylie's son. They are anxious for news of Rose and Oliver happily assures them of her promised recovery. Both men are moved to tears of relief.

At the house, Harry greets his mother and reproaches her for not letting him know sooner of the danger to Rose's life. They speak of his love for the girl and Mrs. Maylie solemnly reminds him that, often, very sincere attachments can be altered by "a wife on whose name there is a stain." Harry counters all of her arguments and declares that he is going to make his feelings known to Rose when she is well enough.

Losberne then welcomes Harry and teases Giles about his marksmanship. He takes Giles aside and informs him privately that Mrs. Maylie has deposited 25 pounds in the bank for him in gratitude for his performance on the night of the robbery.

That evening, there is an atmosphere of relaxation and happiness in the household. The doctor keeps them all amused with stories of his medical experiences and many jokes.

The next morning, Oliver finds the world to be a sweet and beautiful place once more. On his daily walks he is now accompanied by Harry Maylie who gathers an abundance of flowers for Rose. In his studies, Oliver applies himself with increased energy.

His room is at the back of the house, on the ground floor. One day, as he dozes in the warm sunshine, he dreams that he is back in Fagin's room. He imagines that he hears the old man whisper and point at him sneeringly. He awakens in a fright to see the old Jew actually outside the window with the man Oliver ran into at the tavern. The two vanish abruptly as Oliver calls for help.

Commentary

Another new character is added in the handsome presence of Harry Maylie. He is 25 years old and has a frank and easy temperament. In appearance, he resembles his mother.

With his introduction comes a romantic subplot. Harry has been in love with Rose for years and is now anxious to proclaim his affection for her. His eagerness is somewhat tempered by grave warnings from his mother. She does not want to see Rose hurt or disappointed by the generous impulses of a young man.

This romance adds a new element of mystery to the story. When Mrs. Maylie urges her son to "reflect . . . on Rose's history" and to "consider what effect the knowledge of her doubtful birth may have on her," the reader's interest is piqued. It is also worth noting that both Oliver and Rose, who are gentle and sweet-natured, have similar mysterious pasts.

The evil influences that have plagued Oliver in the past are reinserted here with the sinister appearance of Fagin and his scowling companion. Once again, Oliver's security and good fortune are in peril.

CHAPTER 35

Summary

Harry Maylie comes running in response to Oliver's cries. Oliver explains breathlessly and Harry darts over the hedge in quick pursuit of the two felons. Giles and Losberne join the chase. Their search turns up no evidence of the presence or escape of the old Jew and his companion. There are not even footprints in the soft earth. When darkness falls, they reluctantly abandon the pursuit.

For several days, searches and inquiries are made throughout the neighborhood but with no results. Finally, the excitement dies down.

Rose, meanwhile, is returning to health. Her presence within the family once more brings happiness to everyone. Yet, there is a vague tension in the air that is noticeable even to Oliver.

One day, Harry declares his love to Rose. She is pale and tearful as she hears his tender words. He explains that he has loved her for many years and has only been waiting until he has made his fortune before telling her of his affection. Her reply to him is that she is not worthy to be his wife. She describes herself as ''a friendless, portionless girl with a blight'' on her name. She believes she would be a great obstacle to his progress in the world.

Despite many protests from Harry, Rose is firm in her decision. Before he departs, she will only admit that she has very special feelings for him and agrees, finally, to see him again in a year's time or less.

Commentary

Just as Mrs. Maylie had predicted to her son earlier, Rose refuses to become his wife. She is aware of her own shortcomings and will not allow herself to be the cause of disgrace or failure for his family. She is a modest and gentle girl who puts the concerns of others before her own.

As she explains her reasons to Harry, the mystery surrounding her past and her family intensifies. The inexplicable stain on her name prevents her from fulfilling her tender feelings for Harry Maylie. There is only a suggestion at the end of the chapter that these two lovers will have another chance some months from now when Rose has promised to see him again.

The threat to Oliver's safety has diminished with the disappearance of the two criminals. However, the very fact that Fagin is somewhere nearby is an unsettling reminder of his evil power.

CHAPTER 36

Summary

At breakfast the next morning, Harry announces to Losberne and Oliver that he intends to leave in the doctor's carriage. Losberne teases him for having changed his plans so many times in the last couple of days. Harry decides to depart without seeing the ladies.

Taking Oliver aside, Harry instructs the boy to write to him faithfully in London to keep him informed of matters in his mother's house. Oliver is delighted to have such an important assignment.

Glancing briefly at Rose's window, Harry and the doctor set out in the carriage. From the window, unseen, Rose watches his departure and cries softly.

Commentary

From Losberne, the reader discovers that Harry Maylie may be running for political office in the near future. He speaks of the "election before Christmas." Harry will neither confirm nor deny the remark. If the comment is true, it is clear why Rose turned down his offer of marriage. A political life for Harry would expose him to close personal scrutiny and criticism. A wife with any sort of stain on her character would not be an asset to him.

The romantic subplot is temporarily impeded. Rose refuses to accept Harry's offer of marriage. He is returning to London to pursue his career. The only glimmer of hope is in the fact that Harry elicits Oliver's promise to write and keep him secretly informed "whether she — they, I mean — seem happy and quite well."

As Harry sets out for London, Rose watches from her window. Her tears betray more than a sense of sadness at his departure. She is obviously heartbroken at having to refuse his offer of marriage. It seems quite evident that her feelings for him are much deeper than she let him know.

CHAPTER 37

Summary

Bumble and Mrs. Corney (now Mrs. Bumble) have been married for two months. He is sitting dejectedly in the workhouse parlor, reflecting on his unhappiness. He has been promoted to master of the workhouse and no longer wears the dignified clothes of a beadle. In his depression, he considers what has brought about the unhappy changes:

> I sold myself . . . for six teaspoons, a pair of sugar-tongs, and a milk-pot. . . . I went very reasonable. Cheap, dirt cheap!

Unfortunately for Bumble, his wife overhears part of this remark. They fight over who made the greatest sacrifice by marrying the other. Bumble tries to intimidate his wife with the stern look he uses effectively on the paupers, but she only laughs at him. In retort, he makes a comment about her deceased husband. This causes her to utter a loud scream and to break into tears.

Bumble is hardened to this tactic. He encourages her to cry harder because it is good exercise. Feeling satisfied with his victory, he prepares to go out. Mrs. Bumble, who is a veteran of "matrimonial tactics," resorts to a different approach. Knocking off her husband's hat, she attacks him and bestows many blows and scratches on him before pushing him over a chair. Humbled by his wife's persuasiveness, Bumble hastily makes an escape.

In bad humor, Bumble makes a tour of the workhouse. When he hears some female paupers talking noisily in the laundry room, he stops to take out his anger on them. He is startled to find Mrs. Bumble there. To the delight of the women paupers, Mrs. Bumble reprimands him, calls him a fool and sends him away.

In utter humiliation at being degraded in front of the paupers, Bumble goes for a long walk through the streets. When it starts to rain, he enters a tavern where only one other customer is seated.

Bumble contents himself with a drink and a newspaper. Whenever he glances at the other man, who is tall and dark, he finds him returning the look. The stranger remarks that Bumble looks familiar and correctly remembers that he was once a beadle. In the conversation that follows, the man offers Bumble payment in exchange for information about the workhouse. He wants to know about an old nurse who attended a birth 12 years earlier. Bumble informs him that Old Sally died the previous winter. The stranger seems both relieved and disappointed at this news. As he is about to leave, Bumble offers to let him talk to a woman who was with the old nurse when she died. The stranger instructs Bumble to bring that woman to a designated address the next night at nine o'clock. The stranger departs abruptly and Bumble realizes he has no name to refer to. Overtaking the man on the street, Bumble is informed he is called Monks.

Commentary

Bumble is a changed man in many aspects and clearly not pleased about it. His marriage to Mrs. Corney is not a happy one. Each partner regrets having married the other. Bumble is also miserable over losing the symbols of his previous office. With the removal of his cocked beadle's hat and laced coat, Bumble has become ordinary. Dickens remarks facetiously on great men whose stature is derived only from the grand trappings of their positions:

> Dignity, and even holiness too, sometimes, are more questions of coat and waistcoat than some people imagine.

There is a satisfying element of deserved justice in Bumble's altered status. He is a cruel, pompous man who married a woman for her possessions. It is only fitting that this loveless business arrangement should cause him unhappiness. For Mrs. Bumble, as well, it is appropriate since she is as petty and selfish as the man she married.

Bumble's promotion to workhouse master has not been satisfactory for him either. Mrs. Bumble is clearly more the master than he is and does not hesitate to remind him. When she gives him a sound beating and later humiliates him in front of the paupers, Bumble is thoroughly disgraced.

The chance encounter between Bumble and Monks is the real reason for this chapter. Monks' interest in Bumble and the workhouse is a sinister reminder of the danger to Oliver. The fact that Monks is "dusty" and appears to have travelled some distance, suggests that he was Fagin's companion at Oliver's window in Chapter 34.

Monks' inquiries about Old Sally deepen the mystery associated with Oliver's birth. There is added suspense in knowing that Mrs. Bumble has not informed her husband of Old Sally's last words. With the arranged meeting for the next evening, the suspense is heightened.

CHAPTER 38

Summary

The next evening, Mr. and Mrs. Bumble walk hurriedly through the streets to their rendezvous. It is a "dense and sluggish" night and they are dressed in old and shabby garments. They come to a run down area where criminals make their residence. At a rotting building they stop and are greeted roughly by Monks.

A thunderstorm is breaking as Monks leads them inside. The heavy thunder causes him much discomfort and he cringes at the sounds. Upstairs, in a dim room, business is conducted by the capable Mrs. Bumble and Monks. Bumble is nervous and silent as his wife has ordered him to be.

Once they agree on a payment of 25 pounds, Mrs. Bumble discloses what she knows. The two men listen intently as Mrs. Bumble whispers the secret.

Mrs. Bumble was alone with Old Sally. The dying woman spoke of a poor young woman she had robbed 12 years earlier. Before she was able to tell Mrs. Bumble what she had stolen, the old nurse died. But, Mrs. Bumble explains, in the dead woman's hand was a pawn ticket which Mrs. Bumble turned in. She gives Monks a small leather bag containing the pawned merchandise. In the bag is a gold locket containing two locks of hair and a plain, gold wedding-ring. The locket is inscribed with the name "Agnes" and a date, and there is a space for a surname.

Mrs. Bumble asks if any of this information can be used against her. To assure her it cannot, Monks opens a trapdoor in the floor and drops the articles into the river below.

As the Bumbles make their departure, Monks warns them to secrecy about these events. He tells them to forget his name and never to acknowledge that they know him. They agree and depart hastily.

Commentary

The atmosphere and setting in this chapter are appropriate to the nature of the business being conducted. It is an oppressive summer night that promises a violent thunder-storm. The area to which the Bumbles make their way is located near an "unwholesome swamp" where "ruinous" houses stand rotting in the damp air.

In a sinking and tottering old building, the sinister Monks is waiting for them. He leads them into a bare and dim room where the secret is divulged. Mrs. Bumble speaks in a whisper as the two men strain close with rapt attention. Their faces are "ghastly" and marked with "paleness and anxiety." Overhead, the storm breaks and punctuates the tension.

The information that Mrs. Bumble imparts regarding the death of Old Sally does not serve to enlighten the reader. The mystery becomes more complicated with the addition of the gold locket and its strange contents. Further tension is created when Monks takes the only evidence connected to Oliver's past and disposes of it in the river.

The portrayal of the Bumbles in this chapter provides a slight easing of the dramatic tension. Bumble, who is already established as a coward, appears weak with fear in this episode. Mrs. Bumble, on the other hand, is composed and competent in the encounter with the menacing Monks. It is she who enters the building without hesitation and who speaks confidently with Monks. It is also her bargaining powers that secure a substantial reward which, the reader can be sure, she will keep for herself.

Very little more of the mysterious Monks is revealed here. He is seen to be commanding and threatening one moment and, then, frightened and cowering the next. The heavy sounds of the storm cause him great discomfort and he admits to "fits" that overcome him from time to time. As he escorts the Bumbles out of the building, he is startled by every shadow. As soon as they are gone, he summons a boy who has been hiding. Monks has "an invincible repugnance to being left alone."

CHAPTER 39

Summary

The next evening, Bill Sikes wakes up in his usual bad

temper. He is weak from a fever and shabbily dressed. He is now living in different quarters that are much more squalid than his previous residence.

He is attended by his dog and Nancy who looks "pale and reduced." When the girl helps him to get up, he curses and strikes her. She responds by saying that he is unfair to mistreat someone who nursed him through his illness over the past three weeks. She faints from exhaustion.

Fagin arrives just then in the company of the Dodger and Charley Bates. Their combined efforts finally revive Nancy who retires to her bed. Fagin has brought an abundance of food and drink for the ailing Sikes. Sikes is angry at the old Jew for having neglected him over the past weeks. Fagin tries to placate him and agrees to supply him with some money. Sikes insists that Nancy must deliver the money. She gets up and accompanies Fagin and the boys to his residence.

Just as Fagin is about to go upstairs for the money, Monks arrives. At the sound of his entrance, Nancy whisks off her shawl and bonnet and appears to be uninterested in the man's presence. However, when the two men go upstairs, she follows to overhear their conversation. She is first careful to alter her appearance so her shadow will not give her away. Before the men return, she has resumed her place downstairs.

Monks leaves immediately. Fagin comments on Nancy's agitated appearance before giving her the money for Sikes. She departs in great haste. On the street, she sets off in one direction, changes her mind and heads back to Sikes who, because of his illness, does not notice her excitement.

The next evening, Sikes is suspicious of her behavior. She has the "nervous manner of one who is on the eve of some bold and hazardous step." He is not as attentive as Fagin, however, and attributes it to illness. When he asks for his medicine, she adds a sedative to it. Before long, the thief is sound asleep.

It is near ten o'clock as Nancy sets out on her mission. She rushes madly through the streets until she comes to a family hotel near Hyde Park, in the wealthy part of town.

Because of the late hour and Nancy's disheveled appearance, the hotel clerks bar her access to Miss Maylie. After some delay, Nancy sends an urgent message to the young lady. When the clerk returns, Nancy is led upstairs.

Commentary

No explanation is provided for the reappearance of Bill Sikes. He suddenly turns up, plagued by a fever and intense poverty. His life has obviously deteriorated since the night of the fateful robbery. His only friend in his misery is Nancy who has nursed him through his illness. The extent of his insensitivity is revealed when he abuses her in exchange for her efforts.

Fagin's neglect of Sikes illustrates how the old man uses people. An associate in good health and able to be of service is worthy of the old man's attention, but a sick and down-on-his-luck associate is quickly deserted. It is another example of the questionable ethics among thieves.

Nancy's odd behavior with Sikes and at Fagin's house reveals her involvement in the suspicious affairs concerning Oliver. When she spies on Fagin and Monks, it is evident that it was she in Chapter 26 who watched the two men and startled Monks with her shadow. That also explains why she hides her bonnet and shawl when Monks enters.

Nancy's interference in these serious matters reveals once again the compassionate side of her nature. She is taking dangerous risks on Oliver's behalf by spying and by making the visit to Rose Maylie. She is also seen to be clever and resourceful in her undetected efforts to be a spy.

CHAPTER 40

Summary

As Nancy approaches the door of Rose Maylie's room, she feels ashamed of herself and puts on a haughty and careless attitude. When Rose greets her with kindness, Nancy breaks into tears.

Explaining how dangerous her presence here is, Nancy confesses to her involvement in Oliver's criminal associations. She speaks of Monks, whose name Rose does not recognize, and of how he inadvertently provided her with Rose's location. She explains her eavesdropping activities. The first time she heard Monks offer Fagin a reward for recapturing Oliver after he was saved by Mr. Brownlow. He offered even more money if Fagin could thoroughly corrupt the boy into a life of crime. Last night when she listened, she heard Monks declare that all evidence of Oliver's identity had been destroyed leaving Monks in possession of all of the boy's money. He concluded by saying that he still has terrible plans for his "young brother." Nancy warns Rose that Monks plans to demand ransom money from the Maylies if he can get his hands on Oliver.

Nancy is uneasy during her story. When she finishes, she is anxious to get away. Rose pleads to be able to help her, but Nancy refuses. She says it is too late for her to change her life and that she must return to Sikes with whom she is in love.

Rose asks to arrange a further meeting and Nancy agrees to be available every Sunday night on London Bridge. There she will wait for Rose and the person Rose chooses to confide in with this problem. Refusing even a gift of money, Nancy departs. Rose tries to collect her thoughts.

Commentary

The meeting between Nancy and Rose Maylie is an example of effective contrast. Nancy embodies human degradation that is brought about by connections with evil. This is countered by the goodness and sincerity of the angelic Rose Maylie. When Nancy abandons her defiant attitude in the face of Rose's benevolence, Dickens makes it clear that good is triumphing over evil.

Some of the complicated mystery that has been established is unraveled in this chapter. Oliver has an older brother who is the wicked Monks. There is a matter of an inheritance that Monks is eager to possess. He discarded the gold locket in order to destroy evidence of Oliver's identity and to prevent the boy from claiming his "father's will." While the reader is enlightened with regards to Monks' connection to Fagin and Oliver, there is further suspense presented with the knowledge of Oliver's rightful inheritance.

According to Nancy's report of Monks' conversation, the man is desperate and determined to ruin Oliver. Since it is clear that Monks and Fagin know of the boy's whereabouts and his association with the Maylies, the threat to Oliver's existence looms closer.

While Nancy's confession reinforces her inclination to be compassionate, her adamant refusal to repent her ways illustrates the depth of her corruption at Fagin's hands. She declines Rose's offer to be "reclaimed," insisting on her unshakable loyalty to Sikes. She does not want to be responsible for causing the death of the man she loves. In an effort to make Rose understand her feelings, she says:

> When such as I, who have no certain roof but the
> coffin-lid, and no friend in sickness or death . . . set
> our rotten hearts on any man, and let him fill the place
> that has been a blank through all our wretched lives,
> who can hope to cure us?

Nancy is no hardened criminal. She is, rather, an unfortunate, misguided girl who possesses the remnants of human compassion despite her prolonged association with evil. She cannot be blamed for her feelings for Sikes. He has provided her with some measure of human contact that has previously been unknown to her. The worst that can be said of her is that she is weak and susceptible to human emotions.

CHAPTER 41

Summary

Rose spends an anxious night trying to decide on a course of action to help Oliver. She and Mrs. Maylie, accompanied by Mr. Losberne, expect to be in London only two more days before they depart to the coast. In the morning, she determines to write to Harry to request his help in this matter. Composing herself and overcoming her reluctance to contact Harry, she makes 50 painful attempts to begin a letter. Just then she is interrupted by Oliver who is excited. While he was out walking with Giles, he saw Mr. Brownlow enter a house on the Strand. Giles made inquiries and secured the address. Rose immediately sees this as a solution to her dilemma.

Within minutes, she and Oliver are in a carriage bound for Brownlow's. Leaving Oliver in the coach, she is shown in to Mr. Brownlow's study where he is seated with Mr. Grimwig.

The two men are surprised when Rose explains her mission. Grimwig is visibly disturbed by the story and Brownlow is grateful to hear Oliver's name cleared. Rose omits Nancy's story from her narrative, wishing to speak privately to Brownlow about it.

Oliver is then brought in and there is a joyful reunion for him with Brownlow and the ecstatic Mrs. Bedwin. Rose confers in private with Mr. Brownlow and they decide to meet that evening with Mrs. Maylie and Mr. Losberne at the hotel.

Later, when the doctor is informed of the developments, he becomes indignant and eager to act, just as Rose feared he would. Mr. Brownlow, however, is able to placate his impetuosity and suggests a better course of action than setting the law on Fagin's gang.

He reminds Losberne that their combined efforts are for Oliver's benefit. He maintains that the criminals will arrange their own undoing with the law.

Brownlow suggests that they must find a way to trap Monks alone. They will need Nancy's help for this and must wait patiently until Sunday night when they can find her on the bridge. His recommendation is that they pass the five days patiently and not tell Oliver about the events.

Brownlow's level-headedness is accepted by the others. They mutually agree to bring in the assistance of Grimwig and Harry Maylie. Mrs. Maylie adds that she is determined to remain in the city for as long as is necessary and that she will spare no expense on Oliver's behalf.

Before they adjourn, Mr. Brownlow asks for their cooperation regarding his absence from the country. He is not prepared to divulge the reason for his visit to the West Indies yet, but will do so when the time is right.

Commentary

This latest development gathers together the benevolent forces on Oliver's side. The danger to his existence is still very real but, at least, he has the assistance of many good people to counteract the evil threat of Monks and Fagin.

When Rose is talking with Mr. Brownlow, she makes an appropriate summary of Oliver's brief but difficult life:

He is a child of a noble nature and a warm heart . . .
and that Power which has thought fit to try him
beyond his years, has planted in his breast affections
and feelings which would do honour to many who
have numbered his days six times over.

Her sincere belief in the boy is so intense that it even affects the gruff and skeptical Grimwig. He reveals his unseen compassion when he kisses her delightedly while Brownlow is out of the room. Clearly, the old gentleman wanted to believe in Oliver all along.

The inclusion of both Grimwig and Harry Maylie adds to the strength of this campaign for Oliver. By bringing Harry back into the action, Dickens is also creating the opportunity to continue the romantic subplot.

When Oliver is joyfully returned to the good graces of the Brownlow household, Dickens judiciously displays only the tearful reunion with Mrs. Bedwin. He wisely leaves the similarly emotional reunion with Brownlow to the reader's imagination.

Despite the advances that have been made in the unraveling of the complicated mysteries, there is still much that remains undisclosed. Mr. Brownlow's secrecy about his activities out of the country adds to the suspense.

CHAPTER 42

Summary

On the night that Nancy visited Rose Maylie, a young couple approaches the lights of London. The girl carries a heavy bundle on her back while the boy has a small package. They are Noah Claypole and Charlotte. They have been traveling to the city to escape from Mr. Sowerberry whom Charlotte has robbed.

Tired and dusty from their journey, they arrive in a rough section of London. They stop for a meal in a disreputable-looking inn called the Three Cripples. There, they are served by Barney while Fagin eavesdrops on their conversation.

Noah is boasting to Charlotte that he intends to be a gentleman. He plans to accomplish this by becoming "captain" of some street gang of pickpockets.

This is enough for Fagin to hear. He makes his timely entrance and lets Noah know that he has heard of their theft. Using this as leverage, Fagin informs them that he is in "that way of business."

Noah sends Charlotte upstairs with their baggage and talks more with Fagin. Fagin promises to connect Noah with a prominent thief the very next day for the sum of 20 pounds, which is the amount they have stolen from Sowerberry. Noah accepts for himself and Charlotte. He already senses that he is, in some way, in Fagin's power. He requests that he be given "something very light" to do since Charlotte will be so productive. They agree then that he will work "the kinchin lay," which means he will rob young children as they go about on errands for their mothers. When Charlotte returns and is informed of their new line of work, Noah introduces them as Mr. and Mrs. Morris Bolter.

Commentary

The arrival of the two fugitives from the workhouse town of Oliver's birth provides another connection between Oliver's past and his new life in the city. It may seem to be a contrived coincidence on the author's part, but since their contribution is not yet clear, the reader should reserve judgment.

Noah, who is already known to be a cowardly bully, further demonstrates his inferior quality with his treatment of Charlotte. He has her conceal the stolen money so that he will be able to deny his part in the theft if they are apprehended. He allows her to carry the heaviest bundle while they travel and, later, orders her to take all their baggage to the room in the tavern. When Fagin mentions the theft, Noah is quick to blame it completely on the girl. He is also willing to offer her considerable services to the notorious Fagin without first consulting her.

When Fagin finally suggests that robbing children will be a suitable occupation for Noah, the reader must be in agreement. He is a lazy and slow-witted boy suitable for a job that is "sneaking" and "not too trying for the strength."

The fact that Noah and Charlotte seemingly stumble on the very tavern where Fagin is a regular proves that Dickens has additional plans for this couple's involvement in Oliver's fate.

CHAPTER 43

Summary

The next day Noah learns that Fagin is the prominent person who will aid him in his rise to fame. Fagin carefully outlines the criminal philosophy of looking out for "number one." With much difficulty, he is finally able to make Noah understand how it is a rule that applies to all of the thieves.

Fagin then laments the loss of one of his finest pupils. The Dodger has been arrested for stealing a snuff-box. The minimum sentence he will receive is six weeks, but Fagin fears that any additional evidence will make "the Artful nothing less than a lifer."

Charley Bates arrives and is depressed at the Dodger's fate. He says there are witnesses against "lummy Jack" which will probably bring down a life sentence on their best associate.

Fagin and Bates speak glowingly of the Dodger's abilities which impresses Noah. They are convinced that Dawkins will do himself credit at the trial. Fagin wants someone to be present for the Dodger's performance. Noah seems to be the obvious choice since he will not be recognized.

After much persuasion, Noah consents to go. He is dressed as a wagon driver and escorted by Bates to the police station. There, he recognizes the Dodger from Fagin's careful description. The Dodger lives up to his friends' expectations and is belligerent and defiant of the court proceedings. When he is identified by witnesses, the court convicts him and sentences him to life imprisonment for his repeated offences.

Noah joins Charley Bates who is waiting outside and they head back to Fagin's to tell him the news.

Commentary

One of the worst fears that the thieves live with is realized in this chapter. Their lives are made up of poverty, squalor and the scorn of other human beings. They are always hunted and must continually be on their guard against the hangman's noose. Dickens wants it to be clear that there is no glamor or glory associated with their occupations.

The Dodger's life sentence is the first weakening factor in Fagin's insidious network of crime. He has gained new pupils in Noah and Charlotte but has lost one of his most talented thieves.

In the discussion between Fagin and Noah on the fraternity of thieves, the reader is again reminded of the precarious balance that exists in their lives. They are always dependent on each other for continued safety from the law. Yet, there has been more evidence to support the fact that each thief is quite willing to run and forget his fellow man when there is danger. It is a philosophy that is not closely observed.

The trial of the Artful Dodger takes place in a "close and unwholesome" room filled with bored officials and frightened petty criminals. The room is dirty and dusty and there is a "taint" on everything. This is again Dickens' perception of the crumbling institution of justice. It is, as well, a suitable location for criminals to meet the end of their depraved careers.

CHAPTER 44

Summary

On Sunday night, Fagin, Sikes and Nancy are together. The girl has grown pale and thin from her mental struggles over her partial betrayal of the two men. Despite her hatred of Fagin, she is reluctant to be the cause of his downfall.

The two men are discussing business. Both are anxious to make up for lost time and are disappointed that they have no project for this night. As they talk, the church bell strikes 11 o'clock and Nancy casually gets up to go out. When she will not reveal her destination, Sikes refuses to allow her to leave. She becomes hysterical and insistent. He removes her to another room where he detains her by force until the clock rings midnight and she stops struggling.

Sikes and Fagin discuss her recent odd behavior. They agree that it is either an "obstinacy" peculiar to women or "a touch of fever." When Nancy returns to the room, she is calm enough to light Fagin's way out.

Alone with the girl, Fagin confides in her that if she is unhappy with the brutal Sikes, he is willing to help her. He offers himself to her as "a staunch friend."

On his way home, Fagin considers the cause of the change in her. He assumes that she has formed another attachment with a man and is afraid to leave Sikes. He regards this as a wonderful opportunity to dispose of the man he hates and to secure Nancy and her new associate for his own use. He even entertains the idea of getting Nancy to poison Sikes. Assessing her nonchalant reaction when he spoke to her at the door, he assumes he is correct in his evaluation. He resolves to spy on her to discover "the object of her altered regard."

Commentary

Nancy's noticeably changed behavior and appearance are symptoms of the moral struggle she is undergoing. There is a persistent inclination in her for goodness. Despite her own degradation and the malice she bears for Fagin as the cause of it, she cannot bring herself to turn against him.

Caught between her loyalty to these men and her desire to help Oliver, she is suffering the pangs of indecision. When Sikes prevents her from going to her designated appointment with Rose Maylie, she is distressed. Her failure to make the meeting is a moment of great dramatic irony that furthers the tension in the action.

The antagonism between Fagin and Sikes increases in this chapter. Fagin has always been fearful of the other man's power and is eager to find a way to dispose of him. The fact that he is willing to use Nancy to gain what he wants is indicative of his attitude towards his associates. They are instruments that he uses for his own advantages. One moment, he offers Nancy his help and friendship. The next, he is planning to have her spied upon. He advocates the code of honor among thieves yet he is anxious to see Sikes murdered. He will play one against the other to his own end.

CHAPTER 45

Summary
While Noah has his breakfast the next morning, Fagin compliments him on the good work he has done in his new job so far. Next, the old man explains that he has a very special assignment for the boy. Since there is no danger involved for him, Noah agrees to spy on Nancy whenever she goes out.

Six days pass without incident. On the following Sunday, Fagin gets Noah ready. He is sure that Nancy will be going out because Sikes is away. That night, he leads Noah to the Three Cripples where he points out Nancy through a window. When the girl departs from the tavern, they hide themselves from her view. As she moves along the dark streets, Noah is right behind her.

Commentary
When Fagin initiates his ruthless plan, the terrible danger to Nancy and to Oliver and his friends increases dramatically. Even though Nancy is cautious on her way to the bridge, she is unaware of the boy who is following her.

Noah is the natural choice for this job. He has never met

Nancy and so will not be recognized. Furthermore, by his own admission, Noah is "a regular cunning sneak." It is interesting to note that after his very recent discussion with Fagin on the merits of thieves out for each other, the boy misses the irony in spying on one of their own kind.

CHAPTER 46

Summary

Nancy is waiting restlessly on London Bridge near midnight with Noah close by. As the bell strikes 12, a carriage arrives, delivering Rose and Mr. Brownlow. Nancy urges them down some stairs to talk in the protection of darkness. Noah, passing close by, overhears the comment.

Noah hastens ahead of them and hides himself on a landing of the stairs. The others arrive and stop just close enough for Noah to hear their words. Brownlow feels that their location is unsuitable for Rose Maylie, but Nancy defends her choice. She is overcome with fear and apprehension at being detected. Explaining her absence the previous Sunday, Nancy confesses to having drugged Sikes the first time she went to see Rose.

Brownlow explains what she must do. They want to find Monks. If they are unable to secure him, they will need Fagin. Nancy refuses to surrender the old Jew to them. Brownlow agrees that Fagin will come to no harm without her consent.

With their promise that Monks will never know who his informer is, Nancy proceeds to describe the Three Cripples and to outline Monks' routine. Then she provides a detailed description of his appearance. Just as she is about to mention an identifying mark on his neck, Brownlow interrupts and correctly describes the mark. He immediately tries to cover this slip but Noah hears him murmur, "It must be he!"

When Nancy finishes her account and is about to leave, Brownlow and Rose plead with her to give up her lifestyle. They promise her safety. Nancy refuses their offer of assistance and the money they want her to have. Instead, she asks for a small, personal memento from Rose.

Mr. Brownlow and Rose ascend the stairs to return to their carriage. After they are gone, Nancy gives in to her despair and falls crying on the stone steps. When she is able to move away, Noah makes his hasty retreat to inform Fagin of the incident.

Commentary

Freed by the absence of Sikes, Nancy is able to fulfill her promise to meet Rose Maylie on the bridge. Her restless pacing as she waits and her reluctance to speak in an open place betray her extreme agitation.

She reveals the depth of the terrible foreboding feelings she has. She tells her listeners that she has been plagued by:

> Horrible thoughts of death, and shrouds with blood upon them, and a fear that has made me burn as if I was on fire. . . .

She has also imagined seeing coffins in the streets, passing close by her. These are ominous presentiments that alert the reader to the very deadly danger she is in right at this moment as Noah listens.

The description Nancy gives of Monks paints a lurid picture of the sinister man. His features are very dark and, while he is only 26 or slightly more, he is "withered and haggard." His movements are nervous and he is subject to "desperate fits" during which he bites his lips and hands.

It is evident, as Nancy provides these details, that Brownlow is startled and appears to recognize Monks from the description. When she is about to describe a mark on Monks' throat, Brownlow asks abruptly, "A broad red mark, like a burn or scald?" His muttered comment that only Noah hears confirms the reader's suspicion. In some way, Brownlow is acquainted with the man that Nancy is describing. Once more, the mystery deepens.

Brownlow and Rose express their concern and sympathy for Nancy and reveal their innate kindness when they offer to help her in any way they can. Nancy insists that she is past all hope. After securing a remembrance from Rose, the ill-fated girl is left to the mercies of Fagin and Sikes.

CHAPTER 47

Summary

Before the sun is up the next morning, Fagin is sitting in front of the cold fireplace. He is in a terrible rage that causes him to resemble "some hideous phantom, moist from the grave."

Noah is asleep nearby after his adventure the night before. Fagin alternates staring at the boy and at the empty hearth. In his mind, he lists the reasons for his foul temper:

> Mortification at the overthrow of his notable scheme, hatred of the girl . . . an utter distrust of the sincerity of her refusal to yield him up; bitter disappointment at the loss of his revenge on Sikes; the fear of detection, and ruin, and death; and a fierce and deadly rage kindled by all. . . .

Sikes enters, bringing a bag of loot from his night's prowls. When he looks at Fagin, even he is startled by the expression on the old Jew's face.

When Fagin is able to bring himself under control, he asks Sikes what he would do to any one of their associates who turned informer. Sikes describes in vivid detail the brutal treatment he would hand out. Once Sikes' anger and impatience are aroused, Fagin wakes Noah for an account of his activities.

Fagin is so carried away by his fury that he supplies most of the details. The incriminating facts are out and Sikes is uncontrollable in his rage. With a cry of "Hell's fire! . . . Let me go!" Sikes heads for the door. Fagin tries to calm him and pleads with him to be "not too violent for safety."

When Sikes arrives home, Nancy is glad to see him. Then, as she regards the emotion in his face, she is frightened. He tells her that she was watched on the bridge and her words were overheard.

She implores him to spare her life, explaining that she did not turn him in. She begs for her life so that he will not be guilty of murder. With a final effort, she says that they can run away and "lead better lives. . . . It is never too late to repent." But his fury cannot be calmed. Using his pistol, he beats the girl unconscious. As she falls, she holds Rose Maylie's white handkerchief and breathes a final last prayer for mercy. Covering his eyes, Sikes takes a heavy club and kills her.

Commentary

Tension mounts as Dickens reveals the awful depth of Fagin's anger. Realizing the man to be shrewd and ingenious, the reader is also aware of his deadliness. He regards Nancy as a traitor to his thieves' code of honor and will deal with her mercilessly. He cleverly manipulates Bill Sikes into such a fury that her fate is doomed at the hands of the brutal man. When Fagin intercedes and begs Sikes not to be too violent, it is not Nancy's welfare that he is thinking of. He fears detection if Sikes commits murder.

The horrible death of Nancy is portrayed to the reader for several reasons. First, it elicits a sympathetic response for the poor girl who tried to incorporate human emotions into her sterile and unhappy life. It also reveals the depravity of Bill Sikes as he violently takes the life of the only person who was faithful to him. Also revealed is the pervasive effect of the goodness of people like Rose Maylie. The white handkerchief that Nancy clutches as she is struck down becomes a symbol of purity that, unfortunately, didn't reach Nancy in time. It is ironic that Nancy only realizes that repentance can come to them all when it is too late for her.

CHAPTER 48

Summary

As day breaks into brilliant sunshine, Sikes still sits in his room with Nancy's mutilated body. He is horrified by the presence of what he has done. He covers the body with a rug and cannot bear to take his eyes from it. He destroys the club and tries to clean himself and his clothes of the bloodstains. Finally, he backs uneasily out of the house, and departs with his dog.

He wanders aimlessly through the city to the country north of London. All day he moves restlessly about, unable to find a place to rest. Whenever he sees people, he assumes that they regard him "with suspicion." Finally, at nine o'clock, he comes to the village of Hatfield. In a small tavern, he orders food and drink. The townspeople converse easily about everyday trifles until they are interrupted by the arrival of "an antic fellow, half pedlar and half mountebank." This wandering salesman is trying to sell a stain remover. In his eagerness to demonstrate the product, the vendor grabs Sikes' hat and tries to remove the bloodstains on it. Sikes, in guilt-stricken anger, rushes from the tavern and continues his wandering.

Near the local post office, Sikes loiters near the mail coach from London and overhears men talking of the murder of a woman. When the coach departs, Sikes continues on his way.

Traveling alone through the dark night, the murderer imagines that he is being pursued by the ghostly presence of Nancy. His terror mounts when he tries to sleep in a shed and finds he is being watched by the "widely staring eyes" of his victim. When he again takes to the fields, he is glad to come across a fire at a farm. He throws himself into the firefighting activities in an effort to ward off the vision of Nancy.

When morning comes and the "mad excitement" is over, Sikes is again overwhelmed by his fear. He hears the others talking about the murder and learns that he is being sought in the countryside. He determines then to return to the city where he will keep a low profile until he can escape to France with help from Fagin.

As he considers this, he realizes that he may be identified by his dog. He decides to drown the animal but Bull's-eye senses the danger and runs away. Sikes waits for some time but when the dog does not return, he heads alone back into London.

Commentary

With his detailed account of Sikes' activities following the murder, Dickens is revealing the horrible emotional turmoil that overcomes the criminal. At first, he is appalled by his own deed and frightened of the corpse. As he escapes into the country, he feels persecuted and restless. He is unable to find comfort or a place to stop. The news of the murder is already spreading into the countryside and adds to his agitation. When darkness falls, he relives the terrible crime and is haunted by the ghostly presence of his victim. Even the dangerous excitement of the fire is unable to calm the "dreadful consciousness of his crime." When he resolves to kill his dog, he is repeating the ruthless behavior which caused him to murder Nancy. The dog has been his long-time companion but Sikes is willing to dispose of him to save himself from detection. He is a heartless and dangerous criminal and a man devoid of human sentiments.

His decision to return to London reveals the extent of his desperation. He is going to rely on the help of a man who hates him intensely. He is lost and without alternatives. He is Dickens' example of a murderer who cannot escape "justice."

CHAPTER 49

Summary

At twilight, Mr. Brownlow arrives home. He brings with him the notorious Monks who is flanked by two bodyguards. Monks is defiant of Brownlow's authority but is finally intimidated by the old gentleman's determination and ultimatum. Brownlow demands his cooperation or he will be arrested for fraud and robbery.

Alone in the locked room, Brownlow begins the story of how he and Monks — whose real name is Edward Leeford — are connected. Brownlow and Monks' father, Edwin, were close friends. Brownlow planned to marry Edwin's sister but she died. From that time on, Brownlow and Monks' father remained very attached until the latter died.

Monks listens uneasily, unwilling to accept or admit these facts. Brownlow goes on to describe how his young friend was forced into an unhappy marriage that ended in separation. The only child of that union was Monks who, according to Brownlow, was always a "gall and bitterness" to his father. After the separation, Monks' mother went to the continent and completely forgot her younger husband.

Years went by. When Brownlow's friend was 31, he acquired new connections. Monks was about 11 at the time. His father met a retired naval officer who lived alone with his two daughters. The eldest child was a beautiful girl of 19 with whom Monks' father fell in love and pledged to marry.

At this point, Brownlow's friend inherited money from a relative living in Rome. On a trip to collect his inheritance, he fell sick. His estranged wife, who was living in Paris, took her son and traveled to Rome. Edwin died the day after she arrived, apparently leaving no will. All his property went to his wife and child.

This seems to be relieving news to Monks. But Brownlow continues. Before leaving for Rome, Edwin stopped to see Brownlow and left with him a portrait of the naval officer's daughter. He also spoke of providing financially for his legal wife and son before taking up residence outside of England. Brownlow never heard from or saw Edwin again. When he tried to locate the fiancée and her family, they had disappeared.

Then Brownlow recites his discovery of Oliver and of the

circumstances that led him to become involved with the boy. He tells Monks of the striking resemblance of Oliver to the portrait that Monks' father left. When Brownlow failed to recover Oliver from the thieves, he went to the West Indies to locate Monks but learned that he had gone to England. With stubborn determination, Brownlow continued his search until, two hours earlier, he found Monks and brought him home.

When Monks tries to play down the evidence of his half-brother and his share of the inheritance, Brownlow speaks of the gold locket and its contents which Monks disposed of. Monks is disconcerted by how much Brownlow knows. When the old gentleman speaks of connecting him to the murder of Nancy, Monks relents and agrees to sign a statement. He also reluctantly consents to provide for Oliver whom he has defrauded.

At this point, Mr. Losberne enters and excitedly relates that Sikes' dog has been seen and that Sikes is certain to be trapped. Harry Maylie, who helped apprehend Monks, is joining the search. The doctor also speaks of the imminent arrest of Fagin. With this disturbing news, Monks surrenders completely and accepts the conditions of his liberty.

The two men leave Monks in the locked room. Brownlow adds £50 to the reward of £100 already being offered for the capture of the murderer. The men agree to meet two nights later.

Commentary

Brownlow, Losberne and Harry Maylie have been very busy. Their persistence has been rewarded with the "kidnapping" of Monks. This development brings the reader to the critical turning point in the action. The capture of Monks and his confession to having cheated Oliver of his rightful inheritance starts the unraveling of the complicated mystery surrounding Oliver's past.

Many puzzling activities are straightened up in this chapter. The resemblance between the portrait and Oliver is explained, as is the very presence of the painting in Brownlow's house. The reasons for Brownlow's sudden departure from London and for his connection to Monks are clarified. Monks' disposal of the gold locket and the wedding ring into the river was his clumsy attempt to keep Oliver from claiming his inheritance.

Dickens uses the flashback technique to explain the significance of events some 25 years before Oliver's birth. These are essential details of the past that figure importantly in the story of Oliver's life.

Oliver is now recognized to be the child of Mr. Brownlow's good friend, Edwin Leeford, and a beautiful young woman who vanished and somehow ended up in the workhouse. The boy is entitled to a share in his father's will, a fact which Monks was determined to keep hidden.

The promise of capture of Sikes and Fagin adds to the alleviation of Oliver's burdens. There is irony in the fact that Sikes' whereabouts have been located by the presence of the dog he tried to kill. The escape routes for the criminals are being carefully blocked. The hunt for them is closing in.

CHAPTER 50

Summary

Toby Crackit, Tom Chitling and a third criminal, named Kags, are hiding in one of the most vile and secretive parts of London, called Jacob's Island because of its location in an inlet of water. They are anxiously gathered in a room of a crumbling old warehouse. Crackit has selected this location since their other residences have been overtaken by police.

Chitling relates the developments that have befallen Fagin's gang. Fagin and Noah Claypole were arrested that afternoon as Chitling and Bates made their escape. Betsy was brought in to identify Nancy's body. The horrible sight caused her to break down and be removed to a hospital in a straitjacket. The tavern called the Three Cripples has been closed down and all the people in it arrested. Kags, a 50-year veteran of crime and a convict who has returned secretly from a life sentence abroad, predicts that when Noah gives his testimony, Fagin will hang within six days.

Chitling describes the angry mob of people who tried to attack Fagin as he was led away by police. Men and women in a fury pushed aside the officers and "swore they'd tear his heart out."

Suddenly, they hear a noise and Sikes' dog enters. He is dirty and exhausted and falls asleep on the floor. The three fugitives are fearful that the murderer may be on his way. They try to comfort each other by assuming that Sikes has left the country and deserted his dog.

As darkness falls, the three thieves are nervous and apprehensive following the terrible events of the last two days. When a knock is heard, they know who it is by the dog's reaction. With much hesitation, they admit a ghastly-looking Sikes.

They are afraid of him. Sikes demands to know if Fagin's arrest is true. He also wants verified the fact that Nancy's body has not been buried. Charley Bates arrives, and he is repelled by the presence of the murderer. He calls Sikes a monster and vows to turn him in. In his revulsion, Bates attacks Sikes and they wrestle on the floor until Crackit separates them. Sikes locks Bates in an empty room, but his cries for help have already attracted attention. A crowd begins to gather outside the warehouse. Police officers attempt to break down the doors.

Sikes is desperate. He takes a rope and climbs out on the roof. Bates calls to the mob to go to the back of the warehouse. Sikes plans to jump into the water to make his escape, but the tide is out and he sees only a bed of mud. The crowd is triumphant that his escape is impossible. As they surge forward, an old gentleman in the crowd offers £50 if the murderer is taken alive.

Sikes quickly decides to lower himself to the ground, hoping to be able to slip away in the darkness and confusion. He ties the rope to a chimney and is about to put the loop around his chest when he sees an apparition of Nancy's eyes. He loses his balance and drops from the roof. The rope tightens around his neck and he is hanged. The dog, anxious to follow its master, jumps from the roof and attempts to land on Sikes' shoulders. He misses, however, and is killed when his head strikes a stone on the ground below.

Commentary

The setting of this chapter provides a suitable location for the small band of desperate thieves. Jacob's Island is the "filthiest, the strangest, the most extraordinary" area of the city in which only the most destitute take shelter. Here, the remaining members of Fagin's pursued gang have retreated.

The reception that Sikes receives from his associates illustrates the total alienation he has created for himself with the vile murder of Nancy. The outrage of the gathering crowd, both with Sikes and Fagin, reveals the public's opinion of base and depraved criminals. They are contemptuous of thieves and murderers and anxious to see them punished.

The end of Fagin's notorious career is mentioned. He has been arrested and faces certain execution for his life of crime because of the evidence that will be given willingly by the cowardly Noah Claypole. The reader is ironically reminded of Fagin's intense lecture to Noah on the importance of protecting each other. Noah will no doubt have forgotten the words when he testifies at Fagin's trial.

Sikes is the most cutthroat of the criminals and he has committed the worst crime of all. It is only fitting that his death should be presented in full view of the reader. His defiant shout of "I'll cheat you yet!" to the eager mob, is an empty threat. The only person he has cheated is the hangman. The gruesome deaths of Sikes and his dog are poignant reminders of deserved punishment.

Nancy's haunting image is still with Sikes as he tries to escape. It is appropriate that his death is caused by the ghostly appearance of "the eyes again!" Her brutal murder is avenged by his horrible death.

CHAPTER 51

Summary
Two days later, Oliver is traveling in a coach to the town of his birth. He is accompanied by Mrs. Maylie, Rose, Mr. Losberne and Mrs. Bedwin. Mr. Brownlow is following in a carriage with another man.

Oliver and Rose are in a state of anticipation. They have been informed of the developments associated with Monks but are unaware of "the dreadful occurrences that had so recently taken place." Mr. Brownlow and Losberne decided against telling them of the outcome of Fagin's gang.

As they near the town, Oliver is overcome with memories and excitement. His one desire is to be reunited with his dear friend Dick.

Mr. Grimwig greets them warmly when they arrive at the town's best hotel. At dinner, there is an atmosphere of secretive tension. Mr. Brownlow does not join them for the meal, and Losberne and Grimwig go in and out frequently. Even Mrs.

Maylie is called away and returns later with the evidence of tears on her face.

Finally, at nine o'clock, a man is led into the room. Oliver is amazed when he recognizes the man he ran into at the inn and whom he later saw with Fagin at his window. Mr. Brownlow has papers that were drawn up in London and must be supported by Monks' begrudging testimony.

The story is told by Brownlow, interrupted only by Monks' curt summary of details. Oliver is Monks' half-brother, son of Edwin Leeford, Brownlow's friend, and Agnes Fleming, daughter of the naval officer.

Monks attended his father's death. He found two papers which his father dated when he became ill. The first was a letter to Agnes Fleming who was, at this time, several months pregnant. He begs her forgiveness and understanding for his strange explanation for not being able to marry her.

Mr. Brownlow explains the second piece of paper which was Edwin Leeford's will. The dying man had expressed his unhappiness with his legal wife and son and left them an annual sum of £800. The remainder of his estate he bequeathed to Agnes Fleming and their child. A daughter would inherit the estate with no conditions attached. A son, however, was required to prove an unblemished character. The provision was inserted to show the man's confidence in Agnes' "noble nature" which would certainly be passed on to their child. If the expectation was not fulfilled, the legacy would be reverted to Monks.

Monks explains how his mother destroyed the will but kept the letter. Agnes Fleming duly confessed her condition to her father who took his two daughters to live in Wales under a changed name. Agnes, shortly after, left home. Her father, unable to locate her and assuming she was dead, died of a broken heart.

Brownlow takes over the narrative and explains that Monks' mother came to him years later. Her son Edward — Monks — had left home at 18 after robbing his mother. He fled to London where he took up association with "the lowest outcasts." The mother was dying and wanted to find her son. Eventually, he was found and joined his mother in France.

Monks then relates how his mother shared all her secrets with him before she died. She was convinced that Agnes had not died but had given birth to a son. She made her son swear that if he ever found the child, he was to "hunt it down . . . vent upon it the hatred" of their family.

Brownlow now points out to the incredulous listeners that Fagin was well-paid by Monks to secure the moral degradation of Oliver. If the boy were ever rescued, Fagin was to refund part of the money. That is why the two men went to the country to verify Oliver's existence there.

Brownlow now wants to hear the story about the disposal of the locket and ring. Grimwig brings in Mr. and Mrs. Bumble who deny any knowledge of Monks or of the items mentioned. They are proved to be liars when the two old paupers who attended Old Sally's death are brought in. They verify Mrs. Bumble's involvement and add that Oliver's mother was on her way to die at Edwin Leeford's grave when she ended up in the workhouse.

This testimony thoroughly implicates the Bumbles. Brownlow declares his intention to see that they are removed from their positions of trust in the parish. Bumble is as guilty under the law as his wife is. He leaves the room cursing a law that would assume he has any control over his wife.

Brownlow now turns the narrative towards Rose. He asks Monks what happened to the younger sister of Agnes Fleming after their father died. Monks tells them that the child was cared for by some country peasants. Even though Brownlow had failed to locate the child, Monks' mother had. She had warned the simple couple that the child was of "bad blood." As a result, the girl was provided with a miserable existence until Mrs. Maylie rescued her out of pity. Rose, very distressed at this news of her background is affectionately consoled by Mrs. Maylie and Oliver, who is delighted to find that Rose is his aunt.

At this point, Harry Maylie comes in and tells Rose that he, too, has heard this story. He asks her to repeat her denial to marry him. She does but Harry is ready with more news to change her heart. He has broken his former associations with people who would not approve of his marriage with such a woman. He has now only "a heart and home" to offer her. He has given up all rank and privilege to make himself worthy of her. He has become a village minister.

At supper that night, there is much happiness among the company with the news of Rose and Harry's forthcoming marriage. The only tears of sadness are in connection with Oliver's news that his dear friend Dick is dead.

Commentary

All the missing pieces of the novel's puzzles are now filled in. The story, told jointly by a triumphant Mr. Brownlow and a dejected Monks, provides the reader with full enlightenment regarding Oliver's mysterious past. At the same time, the similar mystery concerning the "stain" on Rose's background is clarified.

Everything is coming to its happy conclusion. Oliver has gained his rightful inheritance and knows the full story of his parents. In the process, he has gained a loving and special aunt. The romantic subplot ends on a note of joy as Harry Maylie proclaims his new status in life as a clergyman. Together, he and Rose will embark on a life of happiness.

Virtue and goodness are rewarded, and evil and villainy are denounced. Even the Bumbles receive their just desserts when they are stripped of their jobs and authority. Mr. Bumble is consigned to a worse fate by being left at the hands of his wife.

Yet, in the midst of this joy and unity, comes the sad news that Dick has died. Even in the happy-ending world of Dickens, there is the reminder that nothing can be perfect.

CHAPTER 52

Summary

Fagin's trial is attended by as many people as the courtroom will hold. There is an atmosphere of expectation as the jury withdraws to consider its verdict. While they are out, Fagin is preoccupied with insignificant thoughts about his surroundings. These mental wanderings help him to ward off the "oppressive overwhelming sense of the grave" that looms before him.

The jury returns and declares Fagin guilty. As word of the death sentence passes around, the crowds of spectators roar in approval. When asked if he has anything to say to the court, Fagin only mumbles that he is "an old man — an old man." He is led away to his cell in Newgate to await the fateful Monday.

His thoughts are random and incoherent as he passes the days. He thinks of the men before him who were hanged and how, as he watched, "they changed from strong vigorous men to dangling heaps of clothes!" The reality of his fate closes in on him and he panics with fear. He becomes "so terrible" to behold that the guards are frightened.

On Sunday night, Mr. Brownlow brings Oliver to the prison. They have permission to see Fagin. They find him to be distracted and imagining that he is back with his boys. Fagin finally recognizes his visitors and shrinks away from them with a face "more like that of a snared beast than . . . of a man."

Brownlow makes reference to some papers that Monks entrusted to Fagin. The old man eventually whispers the hiding place to Oliver. Then he asks the boy to help him get away from prison. Oliver is so distressed that he offers to pray with the condemned man. Fagin becomes more crazed and struggles for his freedom. As Brownlow and Oliver leave the cell, they can still hear his shrieking cries.

Oliver must stop to rest before they can return home. He is emotionally depleted from the experience. When they emerge from the prison, it is daybreak and preparations are being finalized for Fagin's execution.

Commentary

The harrowing portrayal of Fagin's last days is a grim reminder of the final reward of a life of crime. Like Sikes, the condemned man is isolated and fearful. In the courtroom, he is the distasteful object of the crowd's scorn and hatred just as Sikes was.

As the day of execution draws closer and Fagin becomes more terrified with the reality of his own death, he is made to face the ultimate degradation. He is no swaggering criminal, facing a glorious end. He is, rather, a snivelling, frightened person. There is no courage or dignity in his final hours. His end is as ignominious as other criminals who have gone before him.

The appearance of Brownlow with Oliver reveals that the boy has since been acquainted with the details of the fate of Fagin's gang. This is a subtle technique by the author to spare the reader any repetition of information. Dickens also wisely omits the actual execution of Fagin from the action. Using the method of contrast, he sets off the brightness and activity of the dawning day against the terrible appearance of "the black stage, the crossbeam, the rope, and all the hideous apparatus of death."

CHAPTER 53

Summary

Before three months have passed, Rose and Harry are married in the little church of which he is now pastor. Mrs. Maylie comes to live with them in their country parsonage.

On Brownlow's suggestion, Oliver agrees to split his yearly income from his inheritance with his half-brother. They hope that this kindness will help Monks to mend his evil ways. He takes his share and moves to America where, after spending all the money, he falls into his habitual life of crime. Later, he dies in prison. Other members of Fagin's gang, who received life transport, also die far from England.

Oliver becomes Mr. Brownlow's adopted son. They move to the country with Mrs. Bedwin to be near the Maylies. Losberne, too, eventually moves to the same area. Even Mr. Grimwig, who has become a good friend to Mr. Losberne, is a frequent visitor.

Noah Claypole receives a full pardon for testifying against Fagin. In keeping with his desire for easy work, he and Charlotte become informers. On Sunday, when taverns are supposed to be closed during church service, one of the pair pretends to faint while the other secures brandy. Then they report the establishment for the sale of alcohol and receive half the fine.

The Bumbles lose their jobs and eventually become paupers in the same workhouse where they once created so much misery. Mr. Bumble is so unhappy that he cannot even rejoice at being separated from his overbearing wife.

The two servants of Mrs. Maylie, Giles and Brittles, also move to the country where they help in running the Brownlow and Losberne households.

Charley Bates is so terrified by the gruesome life and death of Bill Sikes that he abandons his life of crime. With much hard work, he secures himself a contented life as a herdsman in the country.

The lives of Oliver and his worthy companions are spent in continual happiness and peace. In the church where they all worship there is a white marble tablet that bears the name of "Agnes."

Commentary

The novel was actually quite complete when, in Chapter 51, Dickens tied up the loose ends of the mysteries and joined the main characters in a lifelong bond of affection and happiness. However, he continues in this last chapter to distribute just rewards.

The wedding of Harry and Rose Maylie is a conventional happy ending popular in Dickens' day. While the marriage itself is of no direct consequence to the fate of the main character, Oliver, it provides a well-rounded, happy background in which to leave the boy.

The destinies of Oliver's unkind and evil associates are used to illustrate the punishments wrought on wrong-doers. Monks, Noah Claypole and the Bumbles all suffer in proportion to their shortcomings. Only Charley Bates, who chooses to lead an honest life, is spared prolonged misery.

Oliver and his benefactors retire to the country church where they will live out their lives in affection and peace. Dickens makes it clear that they are as happy as any human beings can be in this world:

> I have said that they were truly happy; and without
> strong affection and humanity of heart, and gratitude
> to that Being whose code is Mercy and whose great
> attribute is Benevolence to all things that breathe, hap-
> piness can never be attained.

The monument to Oliver's mother in Harry Maylie's church is a sad reminder of the events that brought these good people together. The white marble tablet is a symbol of the goodness of Oliver's young and ill-fated mother.

Character Sketches

Dickens, like other Victorian novelists, believed that his characters should be part of the total design of the book. He aimed not so much at analysing them as at ensuring that they stood out as vividly as possible. Because of his exceptional powers of observation, coupled with his fascination for the strange, fantastic and grotesque sides of human nature, Dickens was able to create characters that seem both extraordinary and unquestionably real.

In *Oliver Twist* the characters fall into three groups:

(1) those who belong to the "workhouse world"

(2) those who belong to the criminal world.

(3) those who belong to the middle-class world, in which it is Oliver's destiny to find his place.

Apart from the characters in these groups are Oliver and his half-brother Monks. They link all the story's characters together.

Oliver

Oliver, the central character of this novel, is more a symbol than a character. Oliver is the incarnation of innocence. Dickens describes him, significantly, in the opening sentence of the first chapter, as an "item of morality." Dickens says, in the Preface to the Third Edition (1841), "I wished to show in little Oliver the principle of Good surviving through every adverse circumstance and triumphing at last." He felt, and wanted us to feel, deeply moved by Oliver's predicament, rather than by the boy himself, for he stands for every similarly deprived and outcast child.

This is why Oliver seems to be a boy devoid of personality. His behavior is at all times irreproachable, and often unbelievably pious. He does not speak or behave as a boy in his circumstances would. His one clear characteristic, in the early chapters at least, is courage. Because "nature or inheritance had planted a good sturdy spirit in Oliver's breast," he was able to survive the cruel régime of Mrs. Mann's. This spirit is especially clear when he demands, "Please, sir, I want some more." Admittedly he had had the ordeal thrust upon him, by lot, and would have the other boys to reckon with if he failed to perform; still, it must have taken courage, in view of the inevitable fury of the workhouse authorities. Further evidence of Oliver's spirit is seen in Ch. 3, when he resists being apprenticed to Mr. Gamfield; in Ch. 6, when he fights Noah; and in Ch. 7, when he runs away. Once in London, however, he is swallowed up by circumstances. From that time on, as one critic said, "everything seems done to him and for him, and almost nothing is done by him."

In appearance, Oliver is "delicate and handsome." He is in fact the only major character whose appearance is not fully described, except for Rose Maylie (also a representative of "the principle of Good"). Oliver's chief feature is his "expression of melancholy" remarked upon by Mr. Sowerberry and by Toby Crackit, who sees the boy's face as a marvellous asset in the business of thieving: "What an invaluable boy that'll make, for the old ladies' pockets in chapels! His mug is a fortun' to him."

Oliver *looks* innocent because he is innocent. Similarly the villains look villainous. In *Oliver Twist*, appearance coincides with reality. For the same reason, Oliver's speech is the purest King's English, which is hardly to be expected from a boy who has been brought up by, and among, people who are themselves uneducated. Equally improbable is the fact that Oliver's early experiences have not turned him into "either a monster or a wretch."

Everything about Oliver is governed by Dickens' desire to show the survival of that "principle of Good." The boy therefore is little more than a symbol, but he remains nevertheless the novel's focal point.

Monks

Oliver's half-brother, whose real name is Edward Leeford, is bent on depriving Oliver of his share of their inheritance. He employs Fagin to lead the boy astray. Monks can fairly be described as a cloak-and-dagger villain.

When Monks first appears (Ch. 25) he is described only as a "dark stranger." This vague impression persists until Ch. 46, when Nancy gives a more detailed account of his appearance: he is tall, strong, with dark hair and eyes; even his face is dark; his eyes are deeply sunken; he is subject to fits (probably epilepsy) which cause him to bite his lips and hands; he has a "lurking walk" and constantly looks over his shoulder as he goes along. We know more, in fact, about his appearance than about any other aspect of Monks. Apart from the fact that he is completely evil-minded, we are given no idea of the personality as a whole, or of the mind governing his sinister actions.

In his first conversation with Fagin (Ch. 26) he betrays his interest in Oliver — but we do not know that they are brothers until Ch. 40. He is obviously unstable, and subject to uncontrollable fear (shown by his trembling and violent outbursts). One minute he is saying (about Nancy) "Throttle the girl!," and the next minute "I won't shed blood!" We can see that this is a man whose reason is unhinged by some obsession, but what that obsession is does not emerge until near the end of the book.

He is seen by Oliver in the innyard (Ch. 33) when they meet by accident. He is thrown off balance, curses the boy and falls down in a fit. In his meeting with Mr. Bumble and his wife (Ch. 37-8) Monks is in a position of command, and bullies them, yet again he betrays fear easily, and loses his self-control during the storm. When Mr. Brownlow interrogates him (Ch. 49), he is sullen at first, but collapses under the weight of evidence. He is shown throughout to be a coward.

Monks is a device created by Dickens for the purpose of linking the three worlds in which Oliver moves. He and Oliver are the only two characters who have dealings with all three worlds — represented by Bumble, Fagin, and Mr. Brownlow — and they themselves are linked by their blood-relationship. Monks is a key figure in the plot.

Characters of the Workhouse World

Mr. Bumble

Mr. Bumble is the parish beadle in the town where Oliver Twist is born. Hence he has a great deal to do with the manner of Oliver's upbringing — he even invents the boy's name — and is a dominant figure in the first seven chapters. He reappears at intervals throughout the rest of the book, partly to meet the demands of the plot, and partly to supply entertainment. While Bumble is one of the main targets of Dickens' attack, he is also the novel's chief source of comic relief.

Dickens' treatment of Mr. Bumble is heavily ironical. The office of beadle was an inferior position in the parish and Mr. Bumble's self-importance is in inverse proportion to his actual status. Although, to begin with, we see him mainly from the point of view of Oliver or Mrs. Mann, we are soon given a revealing glimpse of the beadle reduced to his proper size ("Compose yourself, Bumble, and answer me distinctly") by the Chairman of the Board and after the galling rebuke "Hold your tongue, Beadle," there can be no further doubt of his true smallness and vulnerability. At the beginning of the novel, he is a pompous swaggering official, by the end he is a pitiful hen-pecked husband. He begins by bullying the paupers, and finally becomes a pauper himself. The decline and fall of Mr. Bumble provide a miniature subplot, in contrast to the progress and victory of Oliver.

Mr. Bumble's appearance is invariably described in terms of his clothing: the official cocked hat, the magnificent coat with its "gilt-edged lapel" and "gold-laced cuff" and the buttons which Mr. Sowerberry admires — which, by a stroke of supreme irony, are embossed with the parochial seal: "the Good Samaritan healing the sick and bruised man" — in which Bumble takes inordinate pride. Without the beadle's coat, plush breeches, cane and cocked hat, Bumble is merely a fat man.

Dickens never allows us, or Bumble, to forget the importance of his cocked hat. It governs every aspect of his behavior. In his conversation with Mr. Sowerberry, he allows himself "precisely as near an approach to a laugh as a great official ought to indulge in;" and when visiting Mrs. Mann "in the full bloom and pride of beadlehood," he takes a chair "not sitting upon or dropping himself into a seat, as any common jacka-napes would, but letting himself slowly and gradually down into a chair." Then he becomes a little too jocular and is recollected: "When Mr. Bumble had laughed a little while, his eyes again encountered the cocked hat; and he became grave."

The parish, which has given him his power, is Bumble's sole sphere of reference. Cold weather is "anti-porochial weather" because more outdoor relief has to be given. Even his marriage seems to him to be an example of "porochial perfection" and it is his failure to penetrate beyond the external, worldly aspect of Mrs. Corney as a future wife, which ultimately seals his doom. By the end of the book, Bumble's eyes have been opened so far that he can question the sanctity of the whole system he once upheld with blind pomposity. When Mr. Brownlow says "You . . . are the more guilty of the two, in the eye of the law; for the law supposes that your wife acts under your direction," Bumble replies "If the law supposes that, the law is a ass — a idiot." Later, when he surveys the workhouse, in his own crestfallen state, he begins to have some glimmering of sympathy for its inhabitants.

Bumble is not a humane man but he is not inhumane either. He is actually moved by Oliver's misery on the way to Mr. Sowerberry's, and he is given pause for a moment by the "earnest manner and wan aspect" of little Dick. But for the most part, he derives considerable pleasure from the exercise of petty cruelty. This is evident when Noah Claypole brings news that Oliver is in trouble, and Bumble has a "gleam of pleasure in his metallic eyes" when he asks for the details. Often a bully will also be a coward. This is true of Bumble, who cannot stand up to his horrible wife.

Through his ridiculous assumption of dignity and power Bumble becomes a comic figure, and this is further heightened by his speech. Officials of local government, however minor their position, do not betray such ignorance, or indeed talk such absolute nonsense, as Bumble often does. Some examples of Bumble's silly statements are: "All public characters, as I may say, must suffer prosecution;" "That outdacious Oliver has demogalized them all!'"; "A porochial life is not a bed of roses, Mrs. Mann." When wooing Mrs. Corney he is at his most fatuous, especially when he speaks of the grim realities of paupers' lives: "That's the way with these people, ma'am; give 'em an apron-ful of coals today, and they'll come back for another the day after tomorrow, as brazen as alabaster." It is, indeed, the very fact that Bumble is a comic figure in a grim world, which makes him an important character in *Oliver Twist*.

Mrs. Mann

Mrs. Mann is the "elderly female" superintendent of the workhouse town's orphanage, in whose charge Oliver spends his first nine years of life. He survives in spite of, rather than because of, her ministrations. She is utterly lacking in humanity. We meet her in only two chapters (Ch. 2 and Ch. 17), in conversation with Mr. Bumble. She is displayed as a hardened hypocrite towards both beadle and children alike. In fact she cannot entirely disguise her hostility towards the children, when she addresses Dick as "you little wretch" — even in Bumble's presence. She habitually embezzles most of the children's allowance. She thrashes the children and locks them in the coal-cellar for presuming to be hungry. Mr. Bumble's verdict "You are a humane woman, Mrs. Mann. . . . You feel as a mother, Mrs. Mann" is yet another example of Dickens' unmitigated irony.

Mr. Gamfield

The chimney sweep to whom Oliver narrowly escapes being apprenticed, Mr. Gamfield is as brutal to his donkey as he is to his apprentices. He "did happen to labour under the slight imputation of having bruised three or four boys to death already" and Oliver, understandably, was terrified at the sight of him.

Mr. Sowerberry

The parish undertaker, Mr. Sowerberry employs Oliver as apprentice, first using him as general house-lad, and then as a hired mourner to walk in the processions of funerals.

In appearance he is tall, gaunt and dressed all in black; "his features were not naturally intended to wear a smiling aspect, but he was in general rather given to professional jocosity." He is the picture of death and poverty — this is Oliver's introduction to the world outside the workhouse.

He is not unkind. In his treatment of Oliver "he was . . . kindly disposed towards the boy." Towards his wife he is habitually deferential.

Mrs. Sowerberry

"A short, thin, squeezed-up woman, with a vixenish countenance," Mrs. Sowerberry is not much improvement on Mrs. Mann, as far as Oliver is concerned. She regards the boy merely as a burden on her household: "I see no saving in parish children, not I, for they always cost more to keep than they're worth."

She controls her husband. In his brief portrait of the Sowerberry household, Dickens casts one of his gloomier sidelights on married life.

Charlotte

A slatternly girl employed by the Sowerberrys, Charlotte's only peculiarity is her blind devotion to Noah Claypole.

She is soft-hearted — when they first meet Oliver she asks

Noah "Why don't you let the boy alone?" — but treats Oliver badly because Noah does. And in the fight (Ch. 6) she supports Noah, although he is the bigger boy. We next meet her in Ch. 27, carousing with Noah while their master is out. She feeds him oysters from a barrel: "I like to see you eat 'em, Noah dear, better than eating 'em myself."

On the road to London (Ch. 42) it is Charlotte who carries all the baggage. After they have joined Fagin, she virtually disappears from the story, but we learn in the last chapter that she remains faithful to Noah and aids him when he goes into business as an informer.

Noah Claypole

A "charity-boy" employed by Mr. Sowerberry, Noah, in contrast to Oliver, is a convincing example of what might be the result of a deprived and poverty-stricken childhood. He is destined for a life of petty crime. At the undertaker's, he persecutes Oliver, not so much through malice as through his need for a scapegoat, having himself been persecuted for so long.

In appearance he is "large-headed, small-eyed, of lumbering make and heavy countenance." (Compare the delicacy of Oliver's looks.) In a book which seeks to expose the miserable consequences of malnutrition, Noah stands out as the one greedy character. Mr. Bumble for example, dines well enough but Noah gorges. He is fed delicacies by Charlotte: the "nice little bit of bacon" in Ch. 5, the oysters in Ch. 27. When he works for Fagin (Ch. 45) he tells him "Don't yer ask me to do anything till I have done eating."

Like that other bully, Bumble, Noah is a great coward. He blubbers when Oliver fights him, and he is always ready to throw the blame on Charlotte. Closely allied with his cowardice is his laziness. He "lolls" in the Sowerberrys' kitchen; he carries only the small parcel to London allowing Charlotte to bear the main bundle; and when he asks Fagin for work, he requests "Something not too trying for the strength, and not very dangerous, you know." He is delighted when Fagin offers him the "kinchin lay." Charley Bates sums up, at first sight, Noah's personality: "The cuttin' away when there's anything wrong, and the eating all the wittles when there's everything right." Noah does not return Charlotte's devotion, but takes pride in it:

"'She's kept tolerably well under, aint she?'' he asked . . . in the tone of a keeper who has tamed some wild animal.''

Despite all Noah's delinquent qualities, he ranks not with the villains in Dickens' gallery but with the victims. He is simply a typical product of the whole system Dickens was attacking. He ends up as the most despised servant of that system for, having turned King's evidence against Fagin, he finally goes into business as an informer.

Dick

Dick is Oliver's "little friend and playmate" at the orphanage. Younger than Oliver, he is depicted as another innocent victim of the parochial system; "the scanty parish dress, the livery of his misery, hung loosely upon his feeble body; and his young limbs had wasted away like those of an old man." Like Oliver, he speaks "correct" English, and displays incredible Christian charity in the midst of his suffering. He invokes God's blessing upon Oliver when they part. Dick is dead when Oliver returns at the end of the story.

Mrs. Corney

The matron of the workhouse where Oliver was born, Mrs. Corney is not introduced until Ch. 23, when Bumble takes tea with her. Avaricious, small-minded and stony-hearted, she is far less sympathetically presented than Bumble. He at least is capable of enjoyment in the performance of his duty, whereas she cannot even enjoy a cup of tea. Her attitude towards the paupers is impatient: 'Some of the old women dying, I suppose. They always die when I'm at meals.'' When she marries Bumble, she is not only shrewish with him in private, but humiliates him publicly. In the nocturnal meeting with Monks, she takes the dominant role and is "to all appearance unmoved (as Mr. Bumble was very far from being) by the strange man's violence.''

The fact that Dickens did not endow either Mrs. Corney or Mrs. Mann with any redeeming features whatsoever, is evidence of the depth of his revulsion of the system they represented.

Old Sally, Anny, Martha

These three women paupers are inhabitants of the workhouse. It is Old Sally who attended Oliver's mother at his birth, and she holds the secret of his parentage until she dies. At her death, Anny and Martha, who call Mrs. Corney to her bedside, listen at the keyhole, thus discovering the secret which they reveal in Ch. 51.

Characters of the Criminal World (including magistrates and police)

Fagin

Fagin is the old man to whom Oliver, on arrival in London, is taken by the Artful Dodger. He is not only a receiver of stolen goods (a "fence"), but also the organizer of a gang of young pickpockets.

Fagin is repeatedly referred to, with heavy irony, as a "kind," "merry," "pleasant" or "playful" old gentleman. This impression is reinforced by his habit of calling everyone "my dear." Oliver, in his innocence, takes several days to become fully aware of the sinister nature of Fagin's business, but the reader sees him as a nightmare figure from the first. Frying sausages over the fire, in the filthy room of a dark house on a slum street, Fagin appears: "a very old, shrivelled Jew, whose villainous-looking and repulsive face was obscured by a quantity of matted red hair."

Dickens made Fagin a Jew, and identified him as "the Jew" throughout the narrative, but this should not be interpreted as anti-semitism. (Dickens was more than once questioned on this point, and, in replying, he drew attention to the fact that Fagin is the only Jew in the story (not counting the insignificant Barney), whereas all the rest of the "wicked" characters are Christians. Fagin is never attacked as a Jew, but as a criminal, a corrupter of youth, a devil incarnate. Dickens simply took it for granted that a typical receiver of stolen goods, in the London of that time, would be a Jew. Fagin's "school" for pickpockets was also a familiar phenomenon to anyone acquainted with the city's underworld; Dickens was not relying on his imagination alone when he created this group of characters.

Fagin's name was, significantly, provided by a boy, Bob Fagin, who had been Dickens' friend and protector in the blacking-factory which loomed so large in his experience. Because of Dickens' mixed feelings about the whole episode of the blacking-factory, it is not surprising to find that he draws upon it when he creates the ambivalent character of Fagin for, in a twisted way, Fagin is Oliver's friend and protector in London — at least in providing the boy with food and shelter — even though he represents all that is most evil in that city.

We never see Fagin in daylight; he is a creature of darkness, who lurks in the streets by night, and spends the day indoors. When Oliver explores his house (Ch. 18) he finds all the windows tightly closed, and "the only light which was admitted, stealing its way through round holes at the top, which made the rooms more gloomy, and filled them with strange shadows." In Ch. 19, when Fagin goes to visit Sikes, "it seemed just the night when it befitted such a being as the Jew to be abroad. As he glided stealthily along, creeping beneath the shelter of the walls and doorways, the hideous old man seemed like some loathsome reptile, engendered in the slime and darkness through which he moved, crawling forth, by night, in search of some rich offal for a meal." The only time he appears by day is at the Maylies', when Oliver is half-asleep and sees Fagin and Monks peering in the window, as if in a dream. But even then it is twilight, and the air has suddenly become "close and confined." Finally at his trial, we see Fagin for the first time in a blaze of light. In his condemned cell, he longs for light, until they bring a candle, but by then Fagin has lost all human identity.

Fagin is described in animal imagery throughout: he is likened to a reptile; Sikes calls him a "wolf", and, when he bites his nails, he discloses among his toothless gums "such fangs as should have been a dog's or rat's." In the condemned cell, when his mind is gone, he rocks from side to side "with a countenance more like that of a snared beast than the face of a man."

Dickens spares no chance to portray Fagin as the most vile and loathsome of creatures, but this is not because Fagin is the true villain of the story: the true villain is the system which fosters such creatures and tolerates such evil. Dickens dwells almost with relish upon the horrible aspects of such characters as Fagin, because he himself is fascinated by them.

The Artful Dodger
Fagin's chief pupil, whose real name is Jack Dawkins, meets Oliver and takes him under his wing. He is an attractive rogue and stands out like a splash of color in the dark underworld.

He is described as being snub-nosed, flat-browed, and he would be an ordinary-looking boy were it not that he "had about him all the airs and manners of a man." He is not more than four feet six inches tall, yet wears a man's coat and hat (even indoors), with the coat-sleeves turned up to free his hands, which he keeps in his pockets. His face is "peculiarly intelligent at all times." In contrast to Charley Bates, he "was of a rather saturnine disposition, and seldom gave way to merriment when it interfered with business." This is not because he lacks Charley Bates' high spirits, but because he is more self-possessed. As Fagin says, "You must get up very early in the morning, to win against the Dodger."

He has no scruples: he is ready to desert a companion if need be (as is seen in Ch. 12, when he leaves Oliver to take the rap for picking Mr. Brownlow's pocket), or to stab Fagin if provoked (Ch. 13). Fagin has taught the boys that their object must be "to take care of number one," and in this as in other matters, the Artful Dodger is his outstanding pupil.

The Dodger's prestige among his associates is great. When they learn he is arrested (Ch. 43) there is general sorrow, not so much because he will almost certainly be sentenced for life, but because it was on a charge of stealing only "a twopenny-halfpenny sneeze-box." Noah Claypole, sent to find out how the Dodger gets on at his trial, is able to bring back the news that "the Dodgers was doing full justice to his bringing-up, and establishing for himself a glorious reputation." As critic Dr. Arnold Kettle points out, this trial is one of the great episodes of the novel: "it re-states in an astonishing form the central theme of *Oliver Twist*: what are the poor to do against the oppressive state?" For "what is so important about the Dodger is not his oddity but his normality, not his inability to cope with the world but his very ability to cope with it on its own terms. Oliver is afraid of the world, the Dodger defies it; it has made him what he is and he will give back as good as he got."

Charley Bates

The Dodger's usual companion, Charley Bates, is described as "very sprightly." He relieves the gloom and tension of Fagin's world with his perpetual tendency to find things uproariously funny. He laughs at Oliver's display of ignorance (Ch. 9); he laughs when he and the Dodger have escaped after picking Mr. Brownlow's pocket (Ch. 12); and on the occasion of Oliver's recapture (Ch. 16), he "laid himself flat on the floor, and kicked convulsively, in an ecstasy of facetious joy." His attitude to their way of life is summed up when he says "it is such a jolly game."

When the Dodger is arrested, Charley is slightly sobered by the sense of the Dodger's fate, but his high spirits are soon restored by Fagin. But the murder of Nancy opens his eyes and when we next meet him (Ch. 50), he is prepared to risk his life to bring Sikes to justice. Of all Fagin's gang, Charley alone escapes the consequences of their crimes and turns to an honest life: "he struggled hard, and suffered much, for some time; but having a contented disposition, and a good purpose, succeeded in the end; and, from being a farmer's drudge, and a carrier's lad, he is now the merriest young grazier in all Northamptonshire."

It is interesting to note that one of Dickens' great friends, the lawyer T.N. Talfourd, was so moved by his treatment of Charley Bates and the Artful Dodger, that he pleaded on their behalf as Dickens was writing the final chapters.

Nancy

A drab (*i.e.* prostitute), Nancy works for Fagin and his associates. Although she plays a large part in the novel, she is not drawn with the same exactitude as the other criminal characters. Two aspects of her nature are brought out strongly: her courage, and her tender heart.

She first enters with Bet (who is a similar character but plays no active role). Their appearance is described from Oliver's point of view: "they wore a great deal of hair, not very neatly turned up behind, and were rather untidy about the shoes and stockings. They were not exactly pretty, perhaps; but they had a great deal of colour in their faces, and looked quite stout and hearty." (Evidence of their habitual gin-drinking.) "Oliver thought them very nice girls indeed. As there is no doubt they were."

In depicting Nancy, more than any other character, Dickens tries to show what she might have been if she had grown up in a different environment. Nancy herself is aware of this, and feels doomed by her past. "Thank heaven upon your knees, dear lady" she says to Rose Maylie, "that you had friends to care for and keep you in your childhood, and that you were never in the midst of cold and hunger, and riot and drunkenness, and — and — something worse than all — as I have been from my cradle. I may use the word, for the alley and gutter were mine, as they will be my death-bed." She blames Fagin: "It is my living; and the cold, wet, dirty streets are my home; and you're the wretch that drove me to them long ago, and that'll keep me there, day and night, day and night, till I die!"

Nancy's humanity is revealed in her kind and, eventually, self-sacrificing attitude to Oliver, in her tragic devotion to Bill Sikes and in such small touches as her compassion for the "fine young chaps" condemned to be hung.

Her courage is revealed in several important episodes: in her defence of Oliver against Fagin and Sikes (Ch. 16); in her decision to seek out Rose Maylie, thereby risking her life (Ch. 40); and in her final refusal to abandon her former companions (Ch. 46) — though this is dictated chiefly by Nancy's fatalistic acceptance of her circumstances: "I am chained to my old life. I loathe it and hate it, but I cannot leave it."

Nancy's speech is worthy of note. Dickens cannot allow her to speak the language of the streets — as he says in the Preface, he aims to present such characters "in all their deformity, in all their wretchedness, in all the squalid misery of their lives" because he sees no reason why they should not figure in a novel "so long as their speech did not offend the ear." Thus he can allow Sikes, Crackit, the Dodger and others to use the slang of their trade but he cannot permit the obscenities and profanity which would certainly have been a major part of Sikes' and Nancy's utterances. Nancy's only vulgar exclamation is the harmless "Never say die!" and Sikes' strongest oath is the improbable "Wolves tear your throats!"

That Dickens himself felt strongly about Nancy is evident by his answer to criticism, again in the Preface to the 1867 edition: "It has been observed of Nancy that her devotion to the brutal housebreaker does not seem natural. . . . It is useless to discuss whether the conduct and character of the girl seems natural or unnatural, probable or improbable, right or wrong. IT IS TRUE."

Bill Sikes

Bill Sikes is a thief and housebreaker who is consistently

represented as brutal. His murder of Nancy provides the climax to the novel. Of him, Dickens says in the Preface, "It has been objected to Sikes . . . that he is surely overdrawn. . . . But of one thing I am certain: that there are such men as Sikes, who, being closely followed through the same space of time and through the same current of circumstances, would not give, by one look or action of a moment, the faintest indication of a better nature." It is debatable whether this is absolutely true of Sikes. Careful study of his behavior reveals more than one such "faintest indication" — most notably in the change which comes over him after the murder of Nancy — but the overwhelming impression is of a savage, coarse, vicious creature who can scarcely be called a man.

He owns a dog (which has "faults of temper in common with his owner"), but nowhere shows any trace of affection towards it. He commands the complete devotion of Nancy, but is equally rough in his manner towards her. In fact he habitually addresses Nancy with "a growl like that he was accustomed to use when addressing his dog." However, he has some respect for her — "She's an honour to her sex" — and he trusts her: "She ain't one to blab," "There ain't a stauncher-hearted girl going." This increases the element of "shock" in his reaction to the news that she has betrayed them (Ch. 47).

His loathing for Fagin is intense. Sikes is the only character who is made to revile Fagin for what he is; Nancy and Charley Bates revile Fagin for what he has done.

Throughout the burglary episode Sikes is rough and threatening towards Oliver, and comes very near to carrying out his threats, but is restrained by Toby Crackit (Ch. 22).

Dickens describes Sikes in strong terms: "savage," "surly,""bitter,""fierce,""harsh,""furious,""desperate." His outward appearance betrays his inner nature. Dirty, unshaven and scowling, he looks like the criminal he is.

After the murder of Nancy, Dickens devotes a whole chapter to the actions, thoughts, and feelings of Sikes as he flees from the crime (Ch. 48). It seems that Dickens was so absorbed in the character, that he identified himself with Sikes; this is borne out by Dickens' obsessive desire (later in his career) to give public readings of this episode. Certainly there is a remarkable difference between the depth of understanding in his portrayal of Sikes, and the emptiness of his portrayal of Monks, for example. Sikes is to be included among those social outcasts with whom Dickens had extraordinary sympathy.

No information is given about Sikes' origin and background — no clue as to how he became the man he is. The same is true of Charley Bates, the Dodger, and all the characters of the underworld.

The end of Sikes (Ch. 50) is among the most powerful pieces of writing in the novel. The central image is not so much Sikes himself, but Jacob's Island — the horrifying scene of his death. But it must be observed that Sikes, at the end, is not merely a hunted animal, but a human being in the grip of terrible guilt; he suffers, in fact, from conscience and thus finally is transformed from brute to man.

Tom Chitling

A minor member of Fagin's gang, callow and slow-witted, Tom Chitling is used mainly as a foil for the Dodger or Crackit. He is introduced in Ch. 18, having just been released from prison. Although older than the Dodger (he is about 18) he is at a constant disadvantage with him. In Ch. 25 we see them playing whist, a card game, and Chitling loses heavily; the Dodger calls him "precious dull" and Charley Bates teases him for being in love with Betsy. In Ch. 50 he brings news of the arrest of Fagin and the others, and is present when Sikes arrives on Jacob's Island.

Toby Crackit

Toby Crackit is a professional and highly skilled burglar. (Notice Dickens' habit of giving many of his minor characters appropriate or descriptive names.) His appearance, in the burglary episode (Ch. 22), is carefully described to give the scene more reality, and to indicate Crackit's personality and standing in the trade — his coat is "smartly-cut," and he is generally something of a dandy.

His chief characteristic is a jaunty self-confidence which is not impaired by the failure of that particular burglary for, when he reappears in Fagin's den (Ch. 25), he looks "tired and worn, but there was the same complacent repose upon his features that they always wore." Only under the final strain of the hunt for Sikes on Jacob's Island, can he not maintain "his usual devil-may-care swagger."

Crackit is highly respected by lesser associates such as Tom Chitling, who thinks it "a creditable thing to have his acquaintance." Towards Oliver, he is kind in an off-hand way, and does restrain Sikes from shooting the boy, but he is the first to suggest abandoning him — true to the criminal rule of "look out for number one" — when they are pursued.

Barney

The waiter at the Three Cripples, Barney is described as "another Jew, younger than Fagin, but nearly as vile and repulsive in appearance." His speech is nasal, probably typical of London Jews of the time. Barney is partly responsible for the management of the burglary at Chertsey. He spots Noah Claypole as a possible agent for Fagin (Ch. 42).

Kags

A "returned transport" — *i.e.* a convict who had been transported overseas as a sentence for criminal activities, and returned illegally, Kags appears only in Ch. 50, where he is introduced presumably to give extra color and atmosphere to the scene of Sikes' death. He is "a robber of fifty years whose nose had been almost beaten in . . . and whose face bore a frightful scar." He had come to Crackit's hide-out on Jacob's Island and is mixed up in the drama by accident. Although a hardened criminal, he is reduced to shivering fear by the events of that day: "Don't leave us in the dark" he begs Crackit.

Mr. Fang

Mr. Fang is the magistrate whom Oliver goes before after he is charged with picking Mr. Brownlow's pocket. He is the sole representative of the legal profession in *Oliver Twist* — except for Mr. Grimwig, who "quitted the bar in disgust" — and Dickens spares no pains in making his brief appearance a memorably unpleasant one.

Mr. Fang is "lean, long-backed, stiff-necked, middle-aged," and his face is "stern, and much flushed." He behaves with gratuitous rage towards everyone in the police office. He is insulting to Mr. Brownlow and would have sentenced Oliver to three months' hard labor had it not been for the bookseller's testimony. Dickens, who sums up the episode by saying that "in such an office as this . . . enough fantastic tricks are daily played to make the angels blind with weeping," drew his portrait of Mr. Fang from a real-life, notoriously harsh magistrate called Mr. Laing, who was dismissed not long after the publication of *Oliver Twist*.

Blathers and Duff

These two Bow Street officers attempt to investigate the Chertsey robbery (Ch. 31). As their names suggest, they are among Dickens' gallery of nincompoops (though he is even more scathing about Bow Street Runners in *Great Expectations*, which he wrote 20 years later). Blathers is the leader. He "walked in . . . and wiped his shoes on the mat as coolly as if he lived there." Duff is more awed by his surroundings. They are pompous about their job, conferring together with great "secrecy and solemnity," but become cheerfully talkative after "a little drop of spirits."

Characters of the Middle-Class or "Benevolent" World

Mr. Brownlow

Mr. Brownlow is the old gentleman whose pocket is picked by the Artful Dodger. After the ensuing confusion, he takes Oliver into his home. It is soon apparent that there is some connection between Oliver and Mr. Brownlow, but it is not disclosed until near the end of the novel that he was a close friend of Oliver's father.

Mr. Brownlow is a respectable, kind, rather absent-minded old gentleman — an example of what George Orwell called "that recurrent Dickens figure, the Good Rich Man." Orwell goes on to say that of course this is a pure dream figure: "Even Dickens must have reflected occasionally that anyone who was so anxious to give his money away would never have acquired it in the first place." This applies rather more to other Good Rich Men than to Mr. Brownlow, perhaps, but it is true that he is a dream figure — a masculine equivalent of a fairy godmother — who appears at exactly the right time (except when Oliver tried to find him, in Ch. 32, but then he was in the West Indies in pursuit of Monks). He eventually adopts Oliver as his own son.

One point of interest about Dickens' "good" characters is their ability, and even their tendency, to shed tears. It is known that Dickens himself was emotionally demonstrative, and would sometimes weep as he wrote. Such freedom of expression is perhaps foreign to most of his readers today but to Dickens it was almost a proof of the ability to feel. Mr. Brownlow is moved to tears, for example, at the mere sight of Oliver (Ch. 12), and has to pretend that he has caught a cold.

Mrs. Bedwin

Housekeeper to Mr. Brownlow, Mrs. Bedwin looks after Oliver when he is ill and becomes very attached to him. She is "a motherly old lady, very neatly and precisely dressed" who teaches Oliver to play cribbage, and tells him stories about her family. When he disappears, and even after Mr. Bumble gives a misleading account of Oliver's life and character (Ch. 17), Mrs. Bedwin refuses to believe it. Her reunion with the boy in Ch. 41 is ecstatic.

Mr. Grimwig

A friend of Mr. Brownlow, Mr. Grimwig is an eccentric and crusty, but fundamentally good-hearted old bachelor. He provides some change of pace and color in the tranquil Brownlow household.

On his first entrance (Ch. 14), Mr. Grimwig is described in great detail — eccentrically dressed, and full of peculiar gestures and grimaces. He "had a strong appetite for contradiction" and therefore will not let himself admit to Mr. Brownlow that he is favorably impressed with Oliver. Similarly, he makes a wager that Oliver will not return when the boy is sent out to the bookstall with a five-pound note. He is perversely glad when Oliver, through no fault of his own, fulfils the prediction.

When Rose Maylie consults Mr. Brownlow in Ch. 41, Mr. Grimwig is "added to the committee," because, as Mr. Brownlow puts it, "he is a strange creature, but a shrewd one" and his legal experience may prove useful. Eventually Mr. Grimwig becomes friendly with his counterpart in the Maylie household — Mr. Losberne — and they enjoy retirement in the country together.

Giles

Butler and steward to Mrs. Maylie, it is Giles who shoots Oliver in the confusion of the burglary, and leads the pursuit and retreat which follow. He is a slightly comic version of one of Dickens' stock types — the trusted family servant — a mixture of honest devotion to duty and inflated self-importance. He is very careful to maintain his dignity in front of the "humbler servants," but he is intimidated by the detectives. At the news of Rose's recovery from her near-fatal illness (Ch. 34), Giles is moved to tears and when, in the same chapter, his mistress rewards him "in consideration of his gallant behaviour on the occasion of that attempted robbery," he enjoys boasting about it to the women servants.

Brittles

A "lad-of-all-work" in the Maylie household, Brittles is always referred to as a boy, and treated as one, although he is over 30 years old. He is slow, and not very intelligent; when interviewed by the detectives, he involves himself and Giles in "a wonderful maze of fresh contradictions and impossibilities" which helps to throw them off Oliver's scent.

Mrs. Maylie

Mrs. Maylie is the owner of the house at Chertsey which is burgled by Sikes and Toby Crackit with Oliver. She is "well advanced in years," and is another benevolent character — not only does she take Oliver in and protect him from being arrested, but also, as is later revealed, she adopted Rose after her father died. Dickens is content to portray Mrs. Maylie in vague and conventional terms.

Rose Maylie

The adopted niece of Mrs. Maylie, Rose eventually turns out to be Oliver's aunt. Her real name is Rose Fleming, Agnes' younger sister. Rose plays an important part in the second half of the novel, and the mystery of the "blight upon her name" adds to the suspense.

She is one of Dickens' idealized pictures of woman: "The young lady was in the lovely bloom and spring-time of womanhood, that age when, if ever angels be for God's good purposes enthroned in mortal forms, they may be, without impiety, supposed to abide in such as hers." She is endowed not only with physical beauty and moral incorruptibility, but also with intelligence and shrewdness. She recognizes, for example, that prison for Oliver would be "the grave of all his chances of amendment."

There is both a contrast and a parallel between Rose and Nancy. The actions of both are determined by their unselfishness: Rose refuses to marry Harry Maylie, and Nancy refuses to leave Bill Sikes, each willing to sacrifice her own chance of happiness (and, in Nancy's case, her own safety) for the sake of the man she loves. Rose protects Oliver from the detectives, and Nancy — as far as she can — protects him from Sikes and Fagin, each supplying a mother's passionate defense for the boy who never knew his mother. When Nancy says to Rose "Oh, lady, lady! If there was more like you, there would be fewer like me," she does not realize how similar they really are. The difference, as Dickens makes clear, lies in their environment. Rose acts out of the security of a well-to-do, middle-class family, whereas Nancy acts out of the misery of the alley and the gutter. Had Mrs. Maylie not adopted Rose, their positions might be far closer.

It is probable that Rose would have died from her illness in Ch. 33, thus greatly simplifying the plot, if Dickens had not been so distressed by the death of his sister-in-law, Mary Hogarth, at the time when that section of *Oliver Twist* was being written. He spoke of his sister-in-law in very much the same way as he wrote of Rose. In her epitaph he wrote: "Young, beautiful and good, God in His mercy numbered her among his angels at the early age of seventeen."

Mr. Losberne

Mr. Losberne is the doctor who is called in to examine Oliver at the Maylies'. He is the counterpart of Mr. Grimwig in the Brownlow household. He is described as having "grown fat, more from good-humour than good living," and he is as "kind and hearty and eccentric an old bachelor as will be found. . . ." His one fault is a marked impetuosity, which deters Rose from seeking his advice (Ch. 41) although he is the family's closest friend.

Harry Maylie

Mrs. Maylie's son, Harry Maylie is brought into the story in Ch. 23, and serves only to provide romantic interest for Rose.

Dickens does not attempt to sketch his character in more than the barest outline.

He is young, handsome, ardent and destined for a brilliant political career. When Rose refuses to marry him, on the grounds that she would harm his "probable advancement to riches and honour," he goes away and sets himself to "level all fancied barriers" between them. When he reappears at the end of the book, he has renounced all claim to power and riches, and has become a clergyman.

Style and Structure

Dickens wrote *Oliver Twist* at great speed. At this period of his life, writing came easily to him. In 1840 he said in a letter "I never copy, correct but very little, and that invariably as I write." Moreover he became absorbed by the story as it developed, and fell upon it "tooth and nail" towards the end. On the other hand, it was written over a period of 18 months, because he was working under great pressure, having taken on several jobs at once.

The first instalment of *Oliver Twist* appeared nine months before *Pickwick* was finished, and Dickens wrote the second half of *Oliver Twist* concurrently with the beginning of *Nicholas Nickleby*. It is hardly surprising that many critics have found fault with the construction of this novel, or that its quality is uneven — though speed of production is only one of many reasons for this — or that a few small threads were left hanging loose at the end. What is more remarkable is the fact that the parts do form a whole; but as Humphry House explains, "the unity of the book derives from impulse and from the energy of its imagination, not from its construction."

To consider how the book is constructed, the novel can be divided into three parts:

(1) Chapters 1-27: The chief characters are introduced, and the two worlds of Bumble and of Fagin are interwoven.

(2) Chapters 28-36: This central section is dominated by the Maylie family, and provides an interlude and added twists to the plot.

(3) Chapters 37-53: The action gathers to a climax and all the characters are brought together.

Section 1

The first seven chapters, devoted to Oliver's early years, are considered by many critics to be the finest part of the book. They contain Dickens' savage indictment of the existing system for "relieving" paupers.

Dickens' chief weapon in these chapters is *irony*, which is contrasted with straight reporting. For example, Chapter 2 begins with a statement of fact: "For the next eight or ten months, Oliver was the victim of a systematic course of treachery and deception." This is followed, a few sentences later, by a shift to heavy irony: "The parish authorities magnanimously and humanely resolved that Oliver should be 'farmed'." Examples of this irony abound in the next few chapters. Mrs. Mann is called Oliver's "benevolent protectress." The Board of Guardians is described as a body of "very sage, deep, philosophical men" whose regulations were "wise and humane." Even the famous watery gruel is a "festive composition."

This sarcasm or irony gains force by its juxtaposition with realism. In the first chapter Dickens paints a terrible picture of the coldness and indifference of the workhouse: Oliver's mother is attended in childbirth by a parish surgeon who "did such matters by contract," and an old woman from the workhouse who "was rendered rather misty by an unwonted allowance of beer." The surgeon's nonchalance towards the dying woman is brought out by contrasting details such as the "great deliberation" with which he puts on his gloves. The same nonchalance is displayed by the priest at the pauper's funeral (Ch. 5), who keeps the mourners waiting in the cold for more than an hour, and is then seen "putting on his surplice as he came along" and reads only "as much of the burial service as could be compressed into four minutes." The whole episode of the pauper's death and funeral shows Dickens' powers, both as a trained journalist and as a social critic.

Dickens also uses caricature to express his views on the social welfare system. This is seen most clearly in the portrait of Mr. Bumble, especially when Bumble is discussing Oliver's rebellion with Mrs. Sowerberry: "'It's not Madness, ma'am,' replied Mr. Bumble after a few moments of deep meditation. 'It's Meat. . . . You've overfed him, ma'am. You've raised an artificial soul and spirit in him, ma'am, unbecoming a person of his condition.'" Here, Dickens is caricaturing the attitude behind the Poor Laws and the ignorance and inadequacy of local officials.

It is worthwhile to give the first seven chapters of *Oliver Twist* an extremely close reading, for they contain the germ of the entire book.

The following nine chapters introduce the world into which

Oliver falls, an underworld dominated by Fagin. These chapters include an interlude in Mr. Brownlow's household, which "seemed like Heaven itself." For the introduction of Fagin and his gang, Dickens uses irony, but the bulk of these chapters are written in a comparatively straightforward narrative style, as the plot gets under way. The police-court episode (Ch. 11) provides another example of Dickens' social criticism, this time without any recourse to irony or caricature.

In Chapter 17, Dickens devotes three paragraphs to a justification of the arrangement of "tragic and comic scenes in regular alternation" which he will be using for the next ten chapters, and to some extent for the rest of the book. For, in interweaving the worlds of Bumble and of Fagin, he is bringing out both the comic and the grim aspects of the same situation — the predicament of the poor in a classified society.

This section culminates in the "expedition" and "burglary" chapters, which one critic has called "one of the most dreamlike" sequences in the novel. Certainly there is a nightmarish quality about the long journey on which Sikes takes Oliver, almost literally at gun-point, starting with the bustle of Smithfield market which Dickens describes in lavish detail, continuing with the cart-rides to unknown destinations and ending with the terrifying loneliness and darkness of open countryside. But the actual burglary is realistic, with much detail about clothes and equipment, the vividness of Crackit's observation of the hall chairs, and the dog. After Oliver has fully entered into the Maylie household the atmosphere again becomes dreamlike.

Throughout this first section of the novel Dickens varies the pace of his story. Some chapters are used mainly to portray character and build up atmosphere, others are used to advance the action. Compare for example Chapters 25 and 26: Chapter 25 does almost nothing but set the scene for what follows, whereas Chapter 26 is complex and swift-moving, with its introduction of Monks and general thickening of the plot. Yet even in this busy chapter, Dickens finds time to insert a paragraph or two of social criticism, in describing the clientele of the Three Cripples.

Section 2

This is the weakest section of the novel. For nine chapters the action is arrested. Oliver sinks gratefully into the comfortable calm of the Maylie household and the only relief is provided by the slightly ridiculous minor characters, Giles and Brittles, Blathers and Duff.

This section completely removes us from the essential conflict. We get glimpses of the sinister background figure Monks, but he is never fully realized. Fagin appears once, but he is seen as a dream-like figure. Dickens devotes much space to praise of Nature and rustic life. We also get a picture of Oliver thriving, studying and pouring out gratitude. "So three months glided away" sums up the smooth monotony of these chapters. Their only value lies in providing the reader with a breathing-space that serves to intensify the acceleration of the dramatic events to come.

Section 3

The final section contains all the elements of the first two for it forces a collision of the unreal Maylie world with the powerful reality of the underworld. It opens with two chapters re-establishing Mr. Bumble's position in the story. He provides a touch of comedy before becoming embroiled with Monks and the intricacies of the plot. The setting then returns to London. For two chapters Nancy is the central figure; two more chapters bring in the Maylies and Mr. Brownlow. The final ten chapters combine all major characters, as the action gathers to a climax (the murder) and its aftermath, in which the facts and consequences are at last sorted out. Those who escape death or imprisonment are accounted for in the conventional epilogue, Ch. 53.

To sum up the features of Dickens' style which have been noted thus far:

(1) Use of *irony*: especially prevalent in the early chapters; used as a means of emphasis and as a form of humor.

(2) Use of *detail*: even when strictly irrelevant, to build atmosphere or character.

(3) Use of *exaggeration* and *caricature*, for emphasis.

(4) Use of *contrast*: between comedy and tragedy, settings, characters and realism and fantasy.

(5) *Variation of pace* from one chapter to another.

(6) Use of *dialogue*: more to portray character and atmosphere than to advance the action.

(7) Use of *recurrent imagery*: for example, images of darkness, suffocation, labyrinths or mazes (of streets, etc.), animal life.

(8) Use of *symbolism:* perhaps unconscious, in a setting or character. The most obvious example of this is seen whenever the weather is mentioned: it is invariably appropriate to the events taking place. For example, the weather is bitterly cold in most of the workhouse chapters, notably when Oliver is born and when Old Sally dies, but in the Maylie chapters there is almost perpetual bright sunshine and warmth; the meeting between Monks and the Bumbles takes place on a "dull, close, overcast summer evening" which ends in a spectacular thunderstorm. Further examples of symbolism may be found in the speech and appearance of the different characters: Oliver speaks "pure" English (even though this, in the circumstances, is highly improbable) because he is pure. The paupers look ugly because poverty is ugly, while the "good" characters are always good-looking.

(9) Use of *description*: Dickens leaves very little to the reader's imagination. Novelists nowadays tend to avoid laboring the point and their method (generally speaking) is comparatively impressionistic. But in the work of Dickens and other novelists of his time, every scene, every state of mind, is described in abundant detail. Where this is not done, the details are omitted purposely, to create a feeling of mystery or suspense. This aspect of Dickens is one of the significant differences of method between Dickens and any comparable writer of our time.

Plot

The weakest aspect of this novel is undoubtedly its plot. Dr. Arnold Kettle calls it "silly and mechanical and troublesome" and points out that the novel itself reveals a "profound and honest" interpretation of life, not through the plot but in spite of it. *Oliver Twist* is not the only Dickens novel to suffer from this disadvantage. George Orwell, in his essay on Dickens, analyses the trouble with what he calls the "awful Victorian 'plot:'" "the typical Dickens novel, *Nicholas Nickleby, Oliver Twist, Martin Chuzzlewit, Our Mutual Friend*, always exists round a framework of melodrama. The last thing anyone ever remembers about these books is their central story." He goes on to say that the melodrama begins as soon as Dickens tries to bring his characters into action: "He cannot make the action revolve round their ordinary occupations; hence the crossword puzzle of coincidences, intrigues, murders, disguises, buried wills, long-lost brothers, etc. etc." Almost all these devices are used in *Oliver Twist*.

Oliver is an orphan and when the novel opens, nothing is known of his parents' identity. But he has a half-brother, Monks, who appears as a sinister stranger halfway through the book. Monks' chief object is to cheat Oliver of his rightful share of their inheritance. The core of the plot is the gradual revelation of this conflict, between Monks and his agents on the one hand, and Oliver (who knows nothing about it) and his friends on the other. The two sides are brought into collision by a series of coincidences:

(1) Fagin, into whose hands Oliver falls when he first arrives in London, is an old associate of Monks, and is therefore easily employed by Monks as a confederate.

(2) Mr. Brownlow, whom Oliver is accused of robbing, happens to have been the oldest friend of Oliver's (and Monks') father.

(3) Rose Maylie, who is living in the house which Oliver is forced to break into, happens to be the younger sister of Oliver's mother.

The full disclosure of these facts is, of course, reserved

until the end of the story although clues and hints are scattered throughout the book.

Several other coincidences help the plot along, for example:

(1) Fagin first learns that Oliver is staying with Mr. Brownlow from the "accidental display" of Oliver's old clothes by the fence who had bought them.

(2) When Mr. Bumble reads the newspaper on his way to London, the advertisement about Oliver is "the very first paragraph upon which his eye rested."

(3) Noah Claypole, after surveying many possible public-houses for a night's lodging, happens to choose the one frequented by Fagin and his friends.

Because coincidence was an accepted convention in 19th century fiction, Victorian readers would be able to swallow these improbabilities more easily than readers can today. One of the most notable features of modern fiction is the unimportance of coincidence to the advancement of the plot. However, there is no doubt that Dickens took far more care with the construction of his later novels than he did with *Oliver Twist*.

One reason for the extreme complexity of *Oliver Twist*'s plot is the fact that Rose Maylie survived her illness in Chapter 33. Dickens had originally intended that she should die but he was so distressed by the death of his own sister-in-law at that time that he was unable to let Rose Maylie die. Since she survived to play a part in the subsequent action, Dickens was obliged to invent some connection between Rose and Oliver, hence the elaborate genealogical tangle without which the plot would be far more digestible.

The careful reader will find, in the course of *Oliver Twist*, several questions which the plot fails to answer. For example:

(1) In Ch. 9, when Fagin is seen gloating over his jewels, special mention is made of one particular trinket "so small that it lay in the palm of his hand," on which there seemed to be a minute inscription. The Jew "pored over it long and earnestly." Did Dickens intend to give this trinket some significance later on? Was it perhaps Agnes' locket? If so, he forgot to explain it.

(2) Fagin's behavior in several episodes is somewhat puzzling — notably in his exchange of looks and signs with Nancy, Ch. 15 — but nowhere more so than in Ch.35, when he (with

Monks) disappears without leaving any footprints. Was it Dickens' intention that this too should be explained later on, or was he so enthralled by the diabolical aspect of Fagin, that he accidentally endowed the old man with supernatural powers?

(3) There is something inconsistent, too, about the burning of Oliver's father's will (as told by Monks in Ch. 51). This will was the only statement of Oliver's right to inherit his father's fortune, on condition that the boy "in his minority should never have stained his name with any public act of dishonour, meanness, cowardice or wrong." If this will had been burnt, why should Monks have been so anxious to involve Oliver in crime? In all probability this is an example of the effect of serial-publication upon the plot: Dickens may have overlooked the implications of earlier chapters, when he came to write the final instalment.

Although these inconsistencies and unnecessary twists of the plot are of some interest to a student of Dickens' method, they are of little importance in a discussion of the plot's weakness. For, as Dr. Kettle explains, "the plot's major fault is that it fails to correspond with the novel's centre of interest or 'essential pattern,'" which is its consideration of the plight of the poor. As he says: "the struggle throughout *Oliver Twist* between the plot and the pattern is indeed a life and death struggle, a struggle as to whether the novel shall live or not. And so far as the plot succeeds in twisting and negating the pattern, the value of the novel is in fact weakened."

Selected Criticisms

If Mr. Dickens were now for the first time before the public, we should have found our space fully occupied in drawing attention to his wit, his invention, his eye for common life, for common men and women, for the everyday aspect of streets and houses, his tendency to delineate the affections and the humours rather than the passions of mankind; and his defects would have served but to shade and modify the praises that flow forth willingly at the appearance among us of a true and original genius. And had his genius gone on growing and maturing, clearing itself of extravagance, acquiring art by study and reflection, it would not be easy to limit the admiration and homage he might by this time have won from his countrymen. As it is, he must be content with the praise of amusing the idle hours of the greatest number of readers; not, we may hope, without improvement to their hearts, but certainly without profoundly affecting their intellects or deeply stirring their emotions.

Spectator (September, 1853).

Even the apparent contrast between Fagin's world and that of Rose Maylie and Mr. Brownlow is not a real one, and this is not because the happy Brownlow world is rendered sentimentally and unconvincingly by Dickens, but because the two do in fact coexist in consciousness: they are the twin sides of the same coin of fantasy, not two real places that exist separately in life. . . . The long burglary sequence, when Sikes takes Oliver down to Chertsey to crack the Maylie house and the two worlds collide at last, is one of the most dreamlike in the novel. Dreamlike too is a later collision, the meeting of Nancy and Rose Maylie in the hotel bedroom — another novelist would make such a confrontation of worlds the most reality-enhancing note in his tale, but in *Oliver Twist* they only confirm the dream atmosphere.

"*Oliver Twist*: Things as They Really Are," by John Bayley.

The tragic-comic mixture is more firmly ingrained in his novels than is sometimes recognized. The obvious place to look for it is in the structure of his books in which we find scenes of dramatic intensity followed by scenes of comedy, a method half-whimsically defended in an introductory chapter in *Oliver*

Twist. This method was no doubt attributable to serial publication, but in Dickens it is a more deeply-rooted device which affects both structure and characterization. One suspects that he would have employed it even if his novels had been published as wholes. His letters indicate that he considered the juxtaposition of serious and comic necessary not only to the reality of the comic character but of the serious character as well. Lear without his fool is not Lear. . . .

The most interesting application of the mixture of genres can be found in . . . his villains. The mixture here is employed not so much between the characters as within the characters. . . . Bumble, Fagin, Squeers, Sampson and Sally Brass, Pecksniff, Uriah Heep, Creakle, Chadband, Podsnap, and other major and minor villains are conceived with gusto and delight. The gusto is apparent in the humor they provoke. They all represent vice or unpleasantness of different kinds, but they all share the characteristic of arousing not only dread but amusement.

"The Poet and the Critics of Probability," by George H. Ford.

A trick of the author's that frightens us today is his fixed epithet for Fagin. This villain is referred to almost exactly three hundred times as "the Jew." After Hitler and Eichmann we can scarcely be expected to find this, to put it as mildly as possible, in good taste, though it can be defended — out of the sensitive context of our times. . . . Nowhere in the description of Fagin is there anything specifically anti-Semitic; nowhere, neither in his physiognomy nor in his gestures nor in his language, is he a caricature — master of caricature though Dickens was — of a Jew. . . . The term "Jew" or its equivalent is never flung at Fagin by Sikes, who despises him, or by anyone else, as a reproach. It is used by the author only (and on one occasion by Oliver), as a means of matter-of-fact identification, a convenient alternative for "Fagin," as "answered" might be a convenient alternative for "said."

"Afterword" to the Signet Classic Edition of *Oliver Twist*.
Afterword by Edward Le Comte

Oliver Twist had a twofold moral purpose: to exhibit the evil working of the Poor Law Act, and to give a faithful picture of the life of thieves in London. The motives hung well together, for in Dickens' view the pauper system was directly responsible for a great deal of crime. It must be remembered that, by the new Act of 1834, outdoor sustenance was as much as possible done away with, paupers being henceforth relieved only on condition of their entering a workhouse, while the workhouse life was made thoroughly uninviting, among other things by the separation of husbands and wives, and parents and children. Against this seemingly harsh treatment of a helpless class Dickens is very bitter; he regards such legislation as the outcome of cold-blooded theory, evolved by well-to-do persons of the privileged caste, who neither perceive nor care about the result of their system in individual suffering. "I wish some well-fed philosopher, whose meat and drink turn to gall within him; whose blood is ice, whose heart is iron, could have seen Oliver Twist clutching at the dainty viands that the dog had neglected . . . . There is only one thing I should like better, and that would be to see the philosopher making the same sort of meal himself, with the same relish." (Chapter IV.) By "philosopher" Dickens meant a political-economist. . . .

The Immortal Dickens, by G. Gissing

Review Questions

1. What is the significance of the following characters or places?
   (a) The Three Cripples   (b) Chertsey   (c) Smithfield
   (d) Mr. Limbkins   (e) Bull's-eye   (f) Jacob's Island
   (g) "Mr. Morris Bolter"   (h) Edwin Leeford
   (i) Agnes Fleming   (j) Saffron Hill.

2. Who is the speaker, and what is the signifance, of each of the following questions?
   (a) "It's all over, Mrs. Thingummy!"
   (b) "Please, sir, I want some more."
   (c) "It's not Madness, ma'am . . . It's Meat."
   (d) "Don't you know the devil when he's got a greatcoat on?"
   (e) "I thieved for you when I was a child not half as old as this!"
   (f) "A beadle! A parish beadle, or I'll eat my head!"
   (g) "He went away, and he *did* die in the streets. There's an obstinate pauper for you!"
   (h) "Every man's his own friend, my dear."
   (i) "I'm an Englishman, ain't I? Where are my privileges?"
   (j) "There's light enough for wot I've got to do."
   (k) "The eyes again!"
   (l) "The law is a ass — a idiot."
   (m) "An old man, my lord, a very old, old man!"

3. By what coincidences is the plot held together?

4. Does Sikes show any "indications of a better nature?"

5. From your reading of *Oliver Twist*, describe:
   (a) the conditions in a typical workhouse of Dickens' time
   (b) a London street scene at that time.

6. Show how Dickens uses:
   (a) food   (b) clothing   (c) furniture to build up character and atmosphere.

7. Discuss the courtship and/or marriages of:
   (a) Mr. and Mrs. Sowerberry
   (b) Mr. and Mrs. Bumble
   (c) Rose and Harry Maylie

8. Find examples of:
   (a) exaggeration   (b) circumlocution
   (c) sentimentality   (d) symbolism

9. Compare the characters of:
   (a) Oliver and Noah Claypole
   (b) The Artful Dodger and Tom Chitling
   (c) Rose and Nancy
   (d) Mrs. Mann and Mrs. Bedwin
   (e) Mr. Grimwig and Mr. Losberne.

10. What parts do the following (unnamed) characters play in the novel?
   (a) "the gentleman in the white waistcoat"
   (b) a traveling tinker
   (c) a bookseller
   (d) "a little ugly hump-backed man"
   (e) "an antic fellow, half pedlar, half mountebank."

Topics for Discussion

1. "Are we to conclude that Dickens' main lesson was that a good heredity can overcome anything, and that in some cases environment counts for nothing at all?" (Humphry House)

2. "*Oliver Twist*, like so much in Dickens . . . is a fantasy of good and evil." (Walter Allen)

3. "'To be thoroughly earnest is everything, and to be anything short of it is nothing.' Dickens' credo about novel-writing is certainly true of *Oliver Twist*." (John Bayley)

4. "Dickens is obviously a writer whose parts are better than his wholes. He is all fragments, all details — rotten architecture, but wonderful gargoyles." (George Orwell)

5. "Dickens . . . shows very little consciousness of the future. . . .

No modern man could combine such purposelessness with such vitality." (George Orwell)

6. "Dickens' figures belong to poetry, like figures of Dante or Shakespeare, in that a single phrase . . . may be enough to set them wholly before us." (T. S. Eliot)

Bibliography

Allen, Walter Ernest. *The English Novel: A Short Critical History*. New York: E.P. Dutton & Co., 1955.

Barnard, Robert. *Imagery and Theme in the Novels of Dickens*. New York: Humanities Press, 1974.

Buckley, Jerome Hamilton. *The Victorian Temper: A Study in Literary Culture*. Cambridge: Harvard University Press, 1951.

Butt, John and Kathleen Tillotson. *Dickens at Work*. New Jersey: Essential Books Inc., 1958.

Cecil, Lord David. *Early Victorian Novelists*. Chicago: University of Chicago Press, Phoenix Books, 1958.

Cockshut, A.O.J. *The Imagination of Charles Dickens*. New York: New York University Press, 1962.

Cruikshank, Robert James. *Charles Dickens and Early Victorian England*. London: Pitman & Sons, 1949.

Davis, Earle. *The Flint and the Flame: The Artistry of Charles Dickens*. Columbia: University of Missouri Press, 1963.

Dexter, Walter. *The England of Dickens*. London: Cecil Palmer, 1925.

Engel, Monroe. *The Maturity of Dickens*. Cambridge: Harvard University Press, 1959.

Fielding, Kenneth Joshua. *Charles Dickens: A Critical Introduction*. London: Longmans, Green & Co., 1958.

Ford, George H. *Dickens and His Readers: Aspects of Novel Criticism Since 1836*. New Jersey: Princeton University Press, 1955.

_____. and Lauriat Lane Jr. (eds.) *The Dickens Critics*. Ithaca, New York: Cornell University Press, 1961.

Forster, John. *The Life of Charles Dickens*. 3 vols. London: Chapman & Hall, 1872-74.

Gissing, George. *Critical Studies of the Works of Charles Dickens*. New York: Greenberg, Publisher, 1924.

_____. *The Immortal Dickens*. New York: Kraus Reprint Co., 1969.

Greaves, John. *Who's Who in Dickens*. London: Elm Tree Books, 1972.

House, Humphry. *The Dickens World*. London: Oxford University Press, 1941.

Johnson, Edgar. *Charles Dickens: His Tragedy and Triumph.* 2 vols. New York: Simon and Schuster, 1952.

Maurois, André. *Dickens.* Translated by Hamish Miles. London: Harper, 1935.

Miller, Joseph Hillis. *Charles Dickens: The World of His Novels.* Cambridge: Harvard University Press, 1958.

Orwell, George. *Critical Essays.* London: Secker & Warburg, 1946.

Pearson, Hesketh. *Dickens: His Character, Comedy, and Career.* New York: Harper & Brothers, 1949.

Pope-Hennessy, Una. *Charles Dickens.* New York: Howell, Soskin, Publishers, 1946.

Price, Martin, ed. *Dickens — A Collection of Critical Essays.* New Jersey: Prentice-Hall, Inc., 1967.

Smith, Grahame. *Charles Dickens: Bleak House.* London: Edward Arnold, 1974.

Wilson, Edmund. *The Wound and the Bow.* New York: Oxford University Press, 1947.

Wright, Thomas. *The Life of Charles Dickens.* London: Herbert Jenkins, Ltd., 1935.

NOTES